SCOT
CAP

JOHN MACKAY

INTRODUCTION

This light-hearted history tells the story of Edinburgh from the earliest times—and consequently also mirrors the development of Scotland as a nation.

The author, although allowing personal opinions to infiltrate about certain characters in our country's history, and apparently unable to repress a strange sense of humour from arising to the surface at the most untoward of times, in the long run keeps to the way of truth. He strays only to raise a smile from time to time and shows us how the story of capital and country are really one.

For example in the very first chapter the formation of the United States of Scotland is hinted at through the man who gave Edinburgh its name. In chapter 4 we go west from Edinburgh with teenage Alexander II, King of Scots to confront the wild Norsemen menacing Scotland's Hebridean seas.

Chapter 5 recounts how Scotland's castles were won back from the English army of occupation; and a few pages on, we have the account of a decisive battle changing the course of this country's history.

In chapter 12 we even go to Westminster and listen to the ambassador to Mary Queen of Scots interviewing Elizabeth the English queen. We tell how the Scottish Crown itself, now safe within Edinburgh Castle, was once buried for years under a church on the north east coast.

Now that it has been made clear that this book was planned to gather together more than just the story of the Capital itself we will give a few words about the illustrations. These are worth more than the usual cursory glance. Although most are intended to be mildly comic many of them have a part in illustrating points on the historical development of the country.

The one in chapter 3 shows the beginning of the growth of the two communities of Edinburgh and of the Canongate, into an eventual whole town and then to a City.

Chapter 7 shows the Castle as it appeared before the building of the Half-Moon Battery (the Battery is illustrated in chapter 14).

And in chapter 18 the illustration shows, not only the jubilant Highlander, but the social niceties of Eighteenth Century Edinburgh in the arrangement of the housing in the tall "lands" or tenements of the time. Note the pig in his stye on the lower ground floor; the labourer on the ground floor; the merchant on the first floor; the lady of means on the second floor and, up top, is the aristocracy.

That drawing expresses a lot in a little space—this book does exactly the same.

EDINBURGH (Scot.Capt)

Front Cover: Edinburgh Castle in the olden time before the Nor' Loch was drained — from a painting by Nasmyth. Reproduced by permission of the National Galleries of Scotland.
Back Cover: Bird's eye view of modern Edinburgh with the Castle and Arthur's Seat prominent landmarks.

"EDINBURGH - The Story Of Scotland's Capital"

Published by Lang Syne Publishers Ltd., 45 Finnieston Street, Glasgow G3 8JU. Printed by Dave Barr Print, 45 Finnieston Street, Glasgow G3 8JU.

© LANG SYNE PUBLISHERS LTD. 1986.

This edition first published by Lang Syne 1986. Reprinted 1994.

Previous editions published by Lang Syne under the title "Scotland's Capital"

First published by Scotprint of Musselburgh from a series in Scotland's Magazine.

ISBN NO. 1 85217 006 9

1

"Before the Beginning"

ABOUT fourteen hundred years ago a procession of weary travellers came straggling past the future site of the Meadowbank International Sports Stadium in Edinburgh. They were heading north-west.

In the van of the procession came a company of scouts on foot—rude warriors with the roving eye. Behind them a body of horse led by a warrior less rude than the others and dressed over all with more than his fair share of ornament. Following this cavalry detachment, more warriors on foot; and trailing in an ever lengthening line of exhaustion in the rear, women and children, the older and weaker having been hoisted on to the lumbering carts, oxen-hauled, which bore the ancient equivelant of the quarter-masters' stores . . .

This little army were Angles from Angleland (England to be) and their leader, the one less rude than the others, a minor king or major chief of the aforesaid Angles, named Edwin. Edwin had territorial ambitions, and was heading north and west with this in view. Now in enemy country and having suffered skirmishes en route, he was keen to find a place to settle and fortify himself.

The westering sun shone on the bearded face of him, accentuating the lines of fatigue, but his eyes were alert. One of his lieutenants rode up and pointed south to where a craggy hill rose to a lion-like head above swamp and forest. Edwin shook his head. He had seen a better place; a long ridge rising to a steep rock to the west; and, skirting that forest land at their left, the Angles passed under the shadow of a long crag and began the ascent of the sloping ridge.

When the head of the procession reached the summit, the weary warriors stood around—or sat down according to their state of exhaustion. And all eyes were fixed on Edwin . . .

Now, while Edwin makes up his mind regarding the suitability of the surroundings for his needs, we take the opportunity to give a brief geography-history explanation of why he had arrived at such a time and in such a place. Let us go back to when Scotland did not exist, except as the weel kent shape more or less as we know it on the map today, to a time when the Romans came north and the resident tribes were named by historians from Rome in this fashion: North of the Firth of Tay, an obscure and widespread mountain peoples dubbed Caledonian : between Forth and Tay, the Maetae : between Forth and Tweed, the Votadini and the Selgovae : and between Clyde and Solway, the Novantes and the Damnonii.

To contain the aforementioned, Hadrian built his Wall from Solway to Tyne. Then slowly pushed north until the Lowland tribes beyond the Wall were subdued.

Hadrian's adopted son Antoninus then built another wall— the Antonine Wall, from Forth to Clyde, for although Occupied Britain now extended to the line between these two last mentioned rivers, the might of Imperial Rome could do nothing with the wild lot farther north. These wild ones with the blood of the Celtic hordes of previous generations coursing within them were given to surprisingly splendid ornament and colourful weaving—the first hint of the Highland costume we know—but inclined to undress for battle, favouring a full frontal charge with their bodies decorated in patterns of red and blue in the manner still favoured by the commoner soldiers of today. Thus in time, when the Roman generals retired to write their memoirs, such volumes as A Roman in the Gloam ın (Campaigns in Darkest Caledonia) and Military Tattoos (The Naked Truth about the North) appeared.

The occupation of what we now call Lowland Scotland did not, however, last much more than a score of years, for troubles were mounting domestically for the Romans and her Legions had perforce to leave Britain to meet invasion of their own homeland.

The Britons had hardly time to get used to the lost feeling of having no occupying force around when they were invaded by the Angles and the Saxons.

The Angles pushed north, forcing the Britons westward and in some instances even across Galloway to Ireland, whose Scots in time were destined to leave Ireland to colonise Argyll—a move inspired by Columba.

Before confusion reigns in the mind of some readers as well as with the Scots finding themselves in Caledonia, let us retrace our footsteps from wandering and rejoin the Angles in the persons of Edwin and his followers as he brooded on the Rock at the summit of the ridge.

As he stood thus, the lowering sunrays turned to a barbaric purple-bronze tone a silhouette of distant mountains to the west. And near at hand below the Rock and to the north, a stretch of water reflected the blue of coming evening. To the south lay a great swamp at the edge of a far-reaching moorland rising to horizon hills.

Edwin nodded in irritation to lettering on a flat boulder announcing: *Tomas Atticinus of the IVth Legion was here,* and one of his minions hastened to scrape off the offending inscription.

Except for a few stones which looked as if they might have formed the basis of some prehistoric fort, no evidence of previous occupation now remained, and Edwin, monarch of all he surveyed, raised his voice: "We stay, and I name this place Edwin's Burgh".

"Edwin's Burgh"—"Edwin's Burgh" . . . the name was passed down the straggling line and the farther it went down that line, so the weaker ones, the tireder ones, the common ones, were careless with the sound of it—were too tired to listen properly, and so "Edwin's Burgh" became "Edin's Burgh" —then "Edin Burgh" and finally "Edinburgh" by the time the end of the line was reached. And, as with other words or groups of words through ensuing centuries, the common folk twisted and slurred them into a popular use. If there had been a "t" in that town title then for sure it would in time have been replaced by an apostrophe and spoken in that fashion nearly all over Sco'land . . .

But one other brief scene was to be witnessed before a rough bedding down for the night took place, against the timber work scheduled for the dawn: above the murmur of talk, a keening wailing voice rose to a crescendo in the dusk. It came

from the ancient sennachie or seer attached to all such folk;
and it screamed, "This place one day will have many people—
a hundredfold than now—a thousandfold, and the ways will be
paved in stone and . . . " here, the aged face became contorted
with the intensity of his prophetic inward vision . . . " and
great bast—great bastions will arise gray to the skies . . . and
the paved ways will in time be scored with double lines of
saffron hue as a magic means to stay these ways from being
jammed and choked to immobility with mot . . . with motor . . .
with motor caaaaaaaars . . . " and with that last strange word,
the contorted countenance went rigid and the ancient fell dead
at Edwin's feet.

" 'Tis as well", observed Edwin dispassionately," for in truth
if we had the likes of him following us around, this history
would indeed have the thunder stolen from it and little need
would there be for the written word, with himself keeping
telling us what was to happen next . . . "

2

"The United States of Scotland"

IN THE previous chapter of this history we told how the company of Angles led by Edwin, came to the Rock at the summit of the ridge and made a fort there which in time was to become the heart of Edinburgh.

Now, once these Angles had settled down, a cautious approach was made to them by the aboriginals of the district— a sparse and scattered company who, discovering that the Angles were inclined to live peaceably, and seeing in the splendid timbered fort that had arisen a protection for themselves should they be allowed to live in the shadow of it, were moved to fraternise.

As time went by, so these aboriginals did nickname the Angles according to the varied natures and characteristics of the newcomers. Thus, the men of the Fort who pestered the aboriginal maidens with their advances were called Try Angles. The good ones were Right Angles, the bad ones Hell's Angles—

and at least one personality who bartered with great cunning was referred to as a cute Angle.

All this time Scotland was spreading from the north-west—from Argyll, then called Dalriada, where the Scots had first settled after leaving Ireland. The hill of Dalriada, once a fort like the one on the Edinburgh Rock, still stands in solemn silhouette above the flat lands through which the Crinan Canal was cut.

The Scots met with an unexpected success here and there in integrating themselves with the native Caledonians, since both had the Celtic strain in them, but the fighting blood was not generally subdued. As tribal kings met each other and fought, as often as not from no more than a natural consequence of meeting, the weaker would lose their land; or, love knowing no boundaries, one tribal chief would marry a rival's sister and in due course their offspring would inherit both territories. This fighting and loving process meant that by about eleven hundred years ago there were roughly—in places very roughly—five states in Scotland.

There were, however, two peoples preventing the United States of Scotland from coming into being: to the south-east that Angleland sometimes called Northumbria which extended north to nearly the Firth of Forth, with Edwin's descendants still holding on precariously to their outpost on the Rock at Edinburgh; and to the north, invading Norsemen or *North*-men were continually trying to gain a foothold in what to them was *South*land (Sutherland).

Sutherland was too far north with all those mountains in between to demand priority of attention, but the south-east with its agricultural and pasture possibilities was another matter, and around A.D. 1000, Malcolm II, the first King of Scots we really know anything of, decided to do something about Angleland. He crossed the lands between Clyde and Forth, marching south to join battle with an Anglo-Danish force which he defeated, and pushed them and Angleland back to the line of the Tweed.

Scotland was taking shape as a nation, with Edinburgh taking shape as its Capital and the Angle's fort on the Rock was now held by Malcolm II's men.

Not that all the Angles went south. Little Angles, descendants of the Edwin Angles, were now part of the

everyday scene. And they talked differently from the Scots.
They talked Anglefield. In turn, their descendants to this day,
talk so. Pockets of them have survived in Blackhall near
Edinburgh and in Bearsden near Glasgow, and Bearsden has
another curious link with the past; a remnant of the Antonine
Wall is still in evidence in the district, if one looks hard
enough . . .

Although Scotland, as mentioned above, was taking shape as
a nation, this did not mean that these United States were
established and their being consolidated within a year or two.
Some might say to this day that the condition of a United
States of Scotland is still an ideal to be striven for but never
realised until professional football is banned.

However . . . after Malcolm II, the succeeding kings
continued the struggle for unity. Some lasted no time at all,
others like Macbeth (no, he wasn't only a Shakespearean
fictional character) actually reigned for seventeen years; but it
was the next Malcolm who broke all records, Malcolm III, who
held to the throne for thirty years.

This Malcolm, sometimes bearing the additional name of
Canmore, which should really be spelt *Ceann Mor*, the Gaelic
for *Big Head*, and no disrespect intended, married a lady
called Margaret, a lady with remarkable family associations.
First of all, one should make it clear that when "Good King
Wenceslas looked out on the Feast of Stephen", the childhood
picture this carol often conjures up is misleading. Apart from
the fact that this writer always understood that "Good King
Wency last looked out", the Feast of Stephen does not mean
that through the window Wenceslas espied a festive board in
the snow groaning under the weight of good things. The
Feast of Stephen means, of course, the Feast Day of St.
Stephen, one time Hungary's legendary and well-loved king.

And just as King Stephen became a saint, so also did
Margaret, Malcolm's queen.

And the family association? *Margaret was a cousin of King
Stephen's wife.*

Margaret has been one of the refugees from an invaded
Hungary, for strange as it may seem, Scotland was not always
the invaded one; sometimes she gave shelter to the oppressed.
Margaret brought to Scotland a personality deeply religious
and for that time, profoundly cultured. To this day such an

early cultural influence is reflected in the little Chapel St. Margaret caused to be built on the Rock of Edinburgh, now the oldest building in the city.

Some may prefer to enshrine Margaret's memory in the Abbey of Dunfermline, whose sturdy Norman pillars also rose at that era of a womanly civilising of Scotland, and this influence being womanly, one's sympathy might not be amiss directed to Malcolm and his men. Many a man of today suffering culture for the wife's sake has been known to wilt in the process. All the more credit then to Malcolm that he went on for thirty years.

3

"The wholly rude and the Holy Rood"

MALCOLM, the third and the best of the four Malcolms of Scotland, not only reigned for an astonishing length of time as mentioned in chapter 2, and stood up fine to his queen's cultural and religious enthusiasms, but also maintained his ability as a fighting man. Indeed he was killed in battle, leading his army to what proved to be a successful thwarting of a Norman invasion, when the son of Duke William of 1066 fame tried to bring Scotland, then tentatively forming into a United States, under his "protection".

And Margaret surely did her part too for the country, for she produced a fine collection of sons, three of whom became kings; and of these, David I commands our attention in particular.

David came to the throne in 1122. The first astonishing disclosure to be made is that he contrived to be friendly with the English—in fact he married the English king's sister. And had emerged triumphant to wear the Scottish crown, despite the practice even then, of certain parties south of the Tweed doing their best to claim same.

David carried on the good work his father and mother had begun in trying to weld Scotland into a nation—a work which had suffered a set back in the years intervening between Malcolm's death and David's accession.

We play history's enlightening beam on David in these formative years for the nation because he it was who began the shaping of Edinburgh of today; in some ways it might be said by accident—or because of an accident—? It happened that one Sunday morning David was persuaded by his courtiers, against the wishes of his priest, to go hunting.

Thus we picture the party, playing truant from the serious observances of life, trotting down the ridge from the Castle (once Edwin's fort) to the forest land under the hill we know as Arthur's Seat—then Crown land, as it remains today.

There followed the excitements of the chase until David found himself separated from the other huntsmen and, dismounting in a glade to rest his horse and stretch his legs, was suddenly aware that, as they say in the thrillers, he was no longer alone . . .

Beside a spring of water, a large stag stood at the entrance to this forest clearing. Then, contrary to the usual inclination of such animals to retreat on sighting or scenting the human kind, it came at the king with a terrifying display of giant antlers, and in the heraldic rampant position knocked David to the ground, prior to dealing what may well have been a fatal blow against the unarmed man.

What follows varies according to who is telling the legend. One version, that David grasped a broken branch lying on the ground and held it up in an attempt to ward off the beast's attack, the branch happening to be shaped like a cross. Another, that the king held the crucifix hanging from a chain around his neck, on high before the stag. And yet one other telling of a sudden appearance in the supernatural manner, of a holy cross between the antlers. Whatever way, a miracle followed: at sight of the Holy Cross (or Holy Rood) the stag reared back and vanished into the trees by the spring.

The spring is still there—"The Spring of the Crucifix"—

just south-east of the site where once stood the Abbey of the Holy Rood, founded by David in thankfulness for his deliverance from the stag. The spring is now enclosed in the well-house named after David's mother Margaret—which well-house was removed from St. Margaret's Well last century from its position at Restalrig when the railway reached that eastern district of the City and vanquished the Well.

The most graphic reminder of the legend of the Stag and the Holy Rood is shown on the gates surrounding the forecourt of the Palace of Holyroodhouse—a stag's head and antlers with a cross between the horns, all in metal. Again, this symbol shows in miniature on the railings surrounding the grounds of the Canongate Kirk: and surmounting the facade of that kirk, a cross is set between real antlers, these appropriately presented by Royalty—appropriately, since the Canongate Kirk has in one sense become the Royal successor as a place of worship to the former Abbey and Chapel Royal beside the Palace.

The name *Canongate* derives from the word *gait* meaning *walk*, but does not refer to any peculiarity in the manner of the good canons of the Abbey of old's pedestrian progress,

but because this *walk* was the way or thoroughfare leading from the Abbey up the ridge.

Now we can see how king David accidentally began the shaping of the Edinburgh of today. His founding of the Abbey formed the nucleus of a community at the foot of the ridge, while the Castle and Royal Palace took shape at the top of the ridge. At that time, the Canongate formed a separate burgh with its Arms that heraldic device of the cross between the antlers (as painted on the side of the Canongate Tolbooth's clock face.)

As the years went by so more folk came to settle under the protective bulk of the Castle on the Rock, while others of a less sectarian persuasion came to live in and around the Abbey precincts.

Thus, we had Edinburgh slowly spreading down the ridge and the Canongate gradually rising up that ridge. One day they were to meet, but meantime we leave them to their separate ways and cannot but help wonder how they got on when their paths crossed in the empty lands between. Did the Canongate crowd, on a lower plane geographically, look down on the ruder and roodless lot higher up ?

4

"Some talk of Alexander"

WHEN DAVID I, the man who founded the Abbey of the
Holy Rood, died, Scotland began to be bothered with boy
kings. His son, the fourth Malcolm was only eleven when he
succeeded to the throne. And from then until the end of
James VI's reign, that is from 1153 to 1625, twelve of the
Scottish sovereigns were 16 or less when they ascended the
throne—or attempted so to ascend.

This succeeding band of teenage or infant monarchs
encouraged rascally Regents ruling; and specialists in intrigue,
treason and statecraft had a field day at times scheming and
experimenting with an early form of the marriage guidance
bureau. Many attempts were made with those exalted
striplings of the male cast, north of the Tweed, to have them
joined in holy matrimony with some Royal lass of the English
court, and the more domineering the lass might be (wearing

the tights as it were—a fashion note that no longer obtains) then the better—for England. And the offspring to maybe rule both kingdoms?

One of our early kings who withstood the pressure was the second Alexander, a sixteen year old who showed that they also matured early, whiles, 700 years ago. He revived for the common good, works that had been fostered by David of Holyrood. He even found approval with the Highland law-unto-themselves chiefs and with that independent-minded south-west corner called Galloway, one day to become the birthplace of John Paul Jones, founder of the American Navy.

But we moved a little ahead there. To return to Alexander's time and *his* navy. One part of Scotland-to-be, the Western Isles, continued irksomely in possession of the roving Norsemen. Alexander, following advice from his better intentioned elders, offered to buy the islands from Haakon of Norway for assuredly these islands were a fine spring-board for the Norsemen should it occur to them to invade the mainland. Haakon refused.

Alexander gathered his Scottish equivelant of the Scandinavian long ships and set out to *take* the islands.

See them, that miniature armada, single-sailed, sweeping the foam of the Western seas behind them as they left the coast of Clyde where distant, the vault and choir of Glasgow Cathedral was building on the hill.

Down and round the Mull of Kintyre, and up north they sailed; then, the expedition facing hopefully now to the west, had to anchor at the Isle of Kerrera out from Oban for the young king was stricken with a fever. And from that fever Alexander died on Kerrera and the venture was cancelled.

Some years later his son the third Alexander turned his attention to the Norse people for invasion was ever more imminent. Alexander III was a meteorological kind of a king, the weather playing an important part in his affairs. Once triumphantly. Once tragically. Triumphantly, when he led his forces against an invading fleet of Haakon's to victory on the Ayrshire shore by Largs—mainly because he had studied weather conditions and chose to challenge the Norsemen to join battle when aforesaid Norsemen would have been better employed keeping well away from that wrecking coast and riding out the storm on the high seas instead of sailing in, to pile up on the rocks with the Scots waiting for them to do just that.

However, all's well that ends well—to a certain extent, for in time Alexander's daughter married Erik of Norway, nicely rounding off peace negotiations which followed the battle at Largs. And when Erik died, the baby daughter of the marriage became Queen Margaret of Norway and heir to the Scottish throne.

Meantime Alexander had married again. This time a French lady called Yolette de Dreux and hopes of a male heir naturally came to mind. But that weather asserts itself in our story again: Alexander, after attending to Court affairs in Edinburgh left, as the day was darkening to night and storm brewing, for his palace in Fife and his lady who awaited him.

When he came to the coast where the Forth makes a narrow passage at the Queen's Ferry (where Saint Margaret once landed on the northern shore for the journey to her well-loved Dunfermline) he was advised not to cross—but did, and remounting, set his horse to the east into the ever increasing storm fury and to the meeting with his young bride.

Folly this was, going on on such a night? With a name like Yolette de Derux coursing through his mind can you blame him?

The weather served him well for his battle with Haakon; ill, it served him for his hoped for meeting, for in the darkness the king lost his way and horse and rider fell to their death over a cliff at a point between where Burntisland and Kinghorn lie on the coast of Fife. The place is marked to this day and quotes lines from a poem of that ancient time proving surely that the common folk looked on him as truly a King of *Scots* as well as of Scotland. Two of the lines run:

>When Alexander our king was dede,
>Our gold was changit into lede . . .

From that place of tragic happening of long ago one can look across the Firth and see the crested silhouette of Edinburgh: and even in Alexander's time, that silhouette was growing apace. The Castle was becoming a fortress proper, a menace to any invader from the east—which may explain why the Norsemen came from the west.

Yes, the Castle at Edinburgh was strong enough now to have been chosen by Alexander as the safest place to keep the Crown Sceptre and Sword of State, symbols of a kingdom, and the predecessors of these symbols of Sovereignty in that Castle today.

Now Margaret the Maid of Norway was to be Queen of Scots but she also died, in Orkney on her way to be crowned in Scotland—a situation of considerable interest to a Royal character who now stalks on to the stage of our story and who had hoped to marry his son to the little Margaret thus allying Scotland with his kingdom which we need hardly say was England, and need we further say whom we are now introducing, since he needs no introduction from the likes of us. Ladies and gentlemen we present much as we would prefer not to, Edward I, King of England, known as "The Hammer of the Scots".

5

"The last of the first Edward"

IS IT NOT a solemn thought that Edward I, King of
England introduced in the preceding chapter as a self-styled
Hammer of the Scots, would have held the Castle at Edinburgh
for much longer than he did, had it not been for an "old sweat"
of the remnants of the Scottish army of that time having
once had a girl friend in the Grassmarket below that famous
Castle? How often thus, when sex rears its diverting head, has
the course of history been equally diverted.

More of that in a moment. How came it that Edward's men
were in the Castle in the first place?

At that time following the tragic happenings in Scotland
previously described, there was quite a collection of claimants
to the Scottish throne; and since the Regents of Scotland could
not agree among themselves—a national failing still obtaining—
they asked Edward I to be the arbiter. Such a decision strikes
one as plain daft. Edward already had his royal warrior's eye
on the Scottish throne, and it must have been that the
aforesaid Regents wished for a denationalisation for their own
ends when they asked Edward to be umpire.

Came the English king to oblige, to Norham at the Border
on Tweedside, surrounded by a brave show of knightly
heraldic splendour to impress and possibly intimidate the
natives. It must have been a trying time for the native
claimants too, for just as after an examination students often
wait for months to learn of results so the claimants, after

Edward heard the reasons of each for claiming the Crown and had departed from Norham, waited long enough; for Edward went into a huddle with himself to contemplate who best would be worst for the throne . . . and so in due course he chose John Baliol a puppet monarch.

The Royal English puppeteer then set about making Scotland into a puppet state—which the Scottish nationalists of the time resented most heartily, they being good at resenting which, like the national failure to agree, still obtains.

This resentment took a practical form. Guerilla warfare began against the English members of the community—a rebellious move that decided Edward to send north an invading and avenging force.

Thus in 1296 the Hammer of the Scots began the hammering. Baliol was deposed. A leaderless Scottish nation was put to the sword and the castles occupied by Edward's men.

A pause here to consider in all fairness, Edward's motives . . .

Suppose you, dear reader, had been the English ruler and furth of your lawful territories there was a small kingdom between Tweed and the Pentland Firth consisting first, of quarrelsome half-breeds north to Tay and then of unknown unnumbered tribes of decorated savages beyond Clyde in the unexplored fastnesses. Would *you* have felt at ease with that across your Border?

Neither did Edward. His mistake was that he overdid things. He took to England the Scottish Crown and Coronation Stone of Destiny—or at least he *thought* he took that last mentioned property, for some say that the Stone is still in Scotland and that it is a more impressive piece than the one taken, in comparatively recent years, back to Scotland from Westminster Abbey for a brief period in our island history.

I digress here to tell of seeing, some years ago, the gentleman who took that Stone from Westminster, standing contemplating Mons Meg within Edinburgh Castle. One of the Castle guides and myself, both having recognised him, were interested in what would be his next move . . . but after a few moments of further contemplation, he walked away, a respectable bowler-hatted figure whom I pointed out as of interest to an Australian lady in the passing who had asked me some direction. She visibly brightened and crowed that I had made her day, herself having been obviously suffering from historical indigestion brought on by a surfeit of the orthodox.

But to return to Edward: he reckoned without Sir William Wallace of Elderslie and Robert Bruce, whose grandfather had been one of the claimants to the Throne at Norham.

Wallace was the man who first rallied the Scots and fired the spark of independence into flame at Stirling, when he defeated an English army by holding his cavalry on the north side of the Forth until Edward's men were advancing across the timber bridging the river and in no position to meet the Scottish charge. For such services to his country Wallace was eventually betrayed by an adherent of the denationalising gang and tried and executed for "treason" in London.

Then Edward, to his considerable exasperation no doubt, died in 1307 without realising his ambition of complete dominance of the Scots, and he was succeeded by Edward II, who was not in the same warrior class at all.

Of Bruce, more in the next chapter, but a word or two on his lieutenants the Lords Randolph and Douglas. They took on the job of winning back the Scottish castles from the army of occupation while Bruce temporarily "took to the heather," he having by this time been crowned King of Scots but being not ready yet to come out into the open.

Among other exploits, Douglas and his men crept across in the gloaming, hooded in black among a herd of kine, until under the walls of Roxburgh Castle, when these dark objects among the genuine grazing cattle suddenly threw off their black cloaks and up went their scaling ladders.

Maybe the biggest job of all fell to Randolph: to recapture the Castle at Edinburgh.

It would seem for this operation that the only possible way was to ascend the rock at a place deemed impossible to climb and thus not specially guarded. At that time the rock descended sheer to the Grassmarket at the chosen point. But how to find a way up?

Enter the aforementioned "old sweat".

In his younger days when stationed inside the Castle with a lawful Scottish garrison, he was wont to leave the barracks at night without signing out at the guard room and without any pass—but with secret passage on a narrow footway down the cliff face, returning by the same route after spending the wee sma' hours in the arms of his lady love in the Grassmarket.

Thus was he chosen to repeat that ascent: to lead Randolph's small band of commandos up the face of the rock by that path once one of love, but of love no longer; and we draw a curtain on what happened to the sleeping garrison within . . .

Now, only Stirling Castle was occupied by the invaders. In the Spring of that year of 1314, Robert the Bruce finished his organising of an army—an army that, like himself, was ready now to come out into the open . . .

6
"All about a battle"

ROBERT THE BRUCE, King of Scots was unique in
various ways—and remains so in this debunking Age, for
he is, *so far*, the only General not debunked by one or other of
the modern historians. None of the young men often fresh from
University, to whom the only link with the second World War
is the overcoat they wore in their student days (the buttons dim
despite its Army or Air Force origin), has yet written of the
Bruce with the searing knowledge brought to bear on the
weaknesses of other military commanders in the field. This
modern eagerness also to debunk pictorially the commanders of,
for example, the Light Brigade of poetic memory, explains
why the Heavy Brigade's successes in the same campaign are
played down—if mentioned at all.

But Bruce is our concern here, not Balaclava.

In an early chapter we mentioned with favour David I,
King of Scots. His son Henry, on marrying, fathered David,
Earl of Huntingdon, whose daughter Isobel wed a Norman,
Robert Bruce by name, who had been given the lands of
Annandale. And their son Robert was named heir to the

throne in 1238, though he never reigned. His son, also Robert married Marjorie, Countess of Annandale, who produced the Robert with whom we are concerned here. Royal blood was there, whatever English Edward had said.

The only important castle now left in the hands of Edward II's men was Stirling. While Randolph had won back Edinburgh Castle, Bruce's brother Edward laid siege to the one at Stirling. A stalemate situation developed where Edward Bruce with his small force could not win a way into the Castle, while the English governor could not get his garrison out. Like sensible men, besieged and besieger met and talked it over. The governor, very likely bored with being stuck on the Stirling rock, had a bright idea: that if he was not relieved by Midsummer Day he would hand the Castle over to the Scots.

Edward Bruce agreed, taking good care that his royal brother was acquainted with this arrangement at the earliest, and the English governor saw to it that Edward II got to know too.

Here then, were two kings both with a splendid excuse to join battle.

As Midsummer Day approached, the Scottish army came together from all quarters of the country to gather under the King's command. He chose a position north of the Bannock Burn where it meandered to the river Forth through a near swamp in places. And with their backs to Stirling's rock Robert the Bruce's men awaited the English host . . .

As I write this, it happens a Press controversy rages briefly on what should be a suitable Scottish National Anthem; and at the same time, on my referring to Burns's poem "Scots, Wha Ha'e," I note the following introduction:

"This song might be accurately described as the Scottish National Anthem. The words, the poet would have us suppose were those in which Bruce addressed his men before the battle of Bannockburn and were fitted by Burns to the air "Hey, tuttie taitie," to which tune it is believed, they marched to battle".

Can one imagine a martial air with a less likely title than "Hey, tuttie, taitie?" But it is of course, the popular tune sung to "Scots, Wha Ha'e," and a good drum-beating metal-clashing tune it is—but would not the words have to be up-dated a bit? One line says: "See approach proud Edward's power". Now all would have been well if this had referred to a certain recent Conservative Prime Minister, but otherwise the line certainly does not fit in today—though assuredly it did on that Midsummer eve of 1314 . . .

We now picture Bruce watching that approach . . .

Not yet weighted in the medieval battle armour of the time, but mounted "on a palfrey low and light," he paces in front of the ranks of his vanguard under the red and gold banner of the Lion rampant; his only defence, a battleaxe.

As the English then wheel to the east to encamp before the battle on the morrow, an English knight, Henry de Boune and a bold man at that, sees this figure on the little horse and further notices the circle of gold on the helmet of its rider.

Thinks the knight: "This is the Scottish king himself—and by himself . . . now what would happen to the morale of the Scots if I challenged and routed him now?"

De Boune without more ado, swings his lance down, pulls his great war-horse round and sets it to thunder across the Bannock Burn and up the slope to where the Bruce now sits his palfrey, static and rock steady . . . but just as the lance comes straight and true to his unprotected chest, so the King suddenly swings his horse round in a dancing curve, stands high in the stirrups and brings his battleaxe down on, and through, the helmet of the English knight as he crashes past.

The battle of the next day was a giant version of that minute conflict, for the mobility of the Scots under a general who was on his own ground and made strategic use of that ground (while yet in command of men less well equipped than their opponents), triumphed over a force greater in number, but unwieldy for that terrain—especially in the ponderous splendour of their cavalry fighting on unfamiliar ground—cavalry that died in the marsh of the Bannock Burn on Midsummer's Day.

Fine it would be to know that this was the decisive battle, but there was still a long way to go. Yet, Bannockburn sent Edward II fleeing over the Border, a retreat of prime importance for Scotland at that time of its resurrection.

A tenuous peace, broken periodically when Border

antagonisms flared, was maintained until the death of Robert the Bruce.

In his last years he granted a charter to Edinburgh making it a Royal Burgh. Six hundred years later, the Duke and Duchess of York (later to be King George VI and his Queen Elizabeth, both descendants of the Bruce) unveiled statues flanking the entrance to Edinburgh Castle of that King of Scots, victor of Bannockburn, and of Sir William Wallace. And there they stand, the freedom fighters, seeming on guard for all time, while the English hordes of today pour across the drawbridge to sight-see, often in a gentle disarming ignorance of their own and anyone else's history.

7

"The Jameses in a jam"

IN 1424 the first Stewart to be called James left for
Edinburgh to mount the Throne as King of Scots. Since
this was over a hundred years after Bruce had caused Edward II
to hie him in haste from Bannockburn, you may well ask (if
your history of Scotland is somewhat rusty) from *where* did
James leave?

Ah well, it's a long story, but it is our duty here to make
such stories succinct.

Robert the Bruce's daughter married Walter Fitzalan, High
Steward of Scotland and their son in time became Robert II—
the first of the Royal Stewarts—or Stewards? Robert II's son
became in due course Robert III and he planned to send *his* son
and heir (christened James for a change) to France. Why?
Because Robert foresaw Crown-grabbing trouble. In these days

it did not need second sight to foresee such trouble in Scotland. And sure enough, trouble arrived on the way to France for young James was captured by pirates and taken before Henry IV of England.

Henry's plans for the boy James was Henry's business, for history—not even this one, can explain why Henry decided to keep James in exile. Perhaps with a view to winning him over to English ways so that James would become an English Nationalist?—and realise latently, Edward the Hammer of the Scots' ambition to see an English monarch on the Scot's Throne? To persuade the boy to stay south and not return to the barbaric north?

Henry, you see, educated James as an English prince would have been. He became a cultured lad—a poet; and, like Robert Burns, burst into verse regarding the ladies, comparing same with aspects of Nature. Thus: ". . . the freshest younge flower, that ever I saw" was written of Joan Beaufort, a high caste English rose.

To counteract the culture, it should be mentioned that James had also developed as an athlete. The picture is complete: an athletic cultured young man with his eye on the beautiful Beaufort—the "tops" in the Beaufort scale.

Had all this to be wasted in dalliance down south? It might have been so, but the Henrys were having troubles of their own; and as Henry succeeded Henry, so their colonial wars across the Channel took up much of their time. Then a calamity comparable to one Scotland was well accustomed to stole up on the English—a minor succeeded to the Throne in the infant person of Henry VI.

The Regent of Scotland and his council asked if they could have their James back.

The English, much distracted with their own State affairs temporarily forgot their eyeing of the northern Throne and agreed. Thus, as we said at the beginning of the chapter, James left for Edinburgh—and yes, he had Joan with him as his Queen.

Into the Scottish Capital they rode—a finely matched couple; and well received they were. As they made for the Castle, James would notice changes. The houses of the Royal Mile were rising higher. Timber was giving way to stone. The first hints of a more enduring covering than thatch appeared on the roofs of the homes of the aristocracy.

(Thatch had its points, nevertheless. After Bruce's death, Edinburgh was periodically harassed by the invader. Bruce's son David II had built the "David Tower" (which more of later) as the centre piece of a formidable curtain of defence for the Castle. Consequently the invaders left the Castle alone and concentrated on setting alight the ever growing huddle of houses now crowning the whole of the ridge all the way down to Holyrood. Following the first few firings, the Edinburgh folk saw to it that an early warning system was instigated, and so, when they heard that the English were on their way, would load their goods and chattels on wagons and temporarily "take to the heather"—and also—and this is the important point, they took their highly inflammable roofs of thatch with them against the time when they would return following the all clear).

Sad to relate that, what would appear to be the beginning of a reign of fairy tale happily-ever-after vintage illustrated by the young couple acknowledging the acclaims of the crowd as the Royal procession rode up to the Castle was nothing more than wishful thinking.

James began, justifiably to throw his weight about a bit. He made new laws. He decreed that—"The fut ball and the golfe be utterly cryit doune" and that men and boys must instead practise archery. Any man who had the nerve to denounce football and golf was surely asking for trouble.

That James was subsequently assassinated in Perth does not imply that a football fan or a golf addict was responsible. Poor James had made enemies among the Highland chiefs in his attempt to bring them into line. James I of Scotland had striven for peace in a warlike way. So did his son James II who would have been better served by Fate if he had kept his men to archery, for he was killed by one of his own cannon bursting at a siege of Roxburgh Castle near Kelso.

James III follows and he too fell foul of his power-grasping lords and was murdered.

And James IV?

He got off to a good start with the Highlands, for he could speak—"the language of the savages who live in some parts of Scotland and in the islands"—the Gaelic in fact. This lively

James had to go to the Highlands half a dozen times before he got these "savages" subdued. The Lord of the Isles was sent to exile in a monastery and, considering this chieftain supreme's previous ploys, his exile must have been a trial indeed.

In the next chapter we will tell how James, who had some knowledge of Latin, French, Italian, Flemish and Spanish as well, tried to find out how the first ever language sounded— by Adam and Eve let us say . . .

8

"Bright and dark days"

NORTH-EAST of the Edinburgh Firth of Forth shore the island of Inchkeith has sent out its lighthouse beam since 1804.

In the time of James IV, Inchkeith was occasionally garrisoned, but often a deserted place—a desert island. He chose it for one of his experiments, setting a deaf and dumb nurse on it, along with two babies to await their first utterances, he, calculating that their speech would be that of the ancient world. Something in the manner of, say, one who was also once sea-surrounded—Noah?

The babies spoke not at all. Maybe if they had been kept there for long enough they would have squawked like sea birds? Or should we believe that, as recorded, they mouthed— "a very guid Ebrew"?

James must not be sneered at for thus experimenting. Beliefs in the power of man to fly be-feathered with no other motive force, and that base metal could be turned to gold in that Age of Alchemy, was but one side of the coin. Real discoveries were afoot. Columbus was discovering America. Edinburgh's gunners were discovering what a doughty cannon Mons Meg had turned out to be. Messrs. Chepman and Myllar were discovering that their first printing shop off the Royal Mile was drawing the crowds—and James as their sponsor, naturally also came to see, for he was in the vanguard of a little renaissance—a brief Golden Age for Scotland. He caused the guest house by the Abbey at the foot of the Canongate to be transformed into a Palace—the Palace of Holyroodhouse—the twin towers to the north of the forecourt of today being partly of James's time.

He also encouraged the arts and the chivalry of the tournament and created the first and formidable proudly pennanted Scottish navy, chasing the English pirates from the Forth (his own sailors not being averse to piracy themselves when it suited). In 1496 he decreed that all landowners must send their sons to be taught Latin and to university to study law. His Royal title is perpetuated in King's College, Aberdeen, and he was also the founder of the now far-famed College of Surgeons in Edinburgh.

An adventurous and brave man and some say, the worthiest king of Europe of his time.

Henry VII respected this new northern force enough to forget about any thought of invasion and instead, offered his daughter Margaret in marriage to James—plus a peace treaty.

In 1503 Margaret came to Scotland with her retinue, met beyond the City border by James on his charger on whose broad beam, it is said he set as pillion, his bride to be.

Thirteen she was at the time, a young Tudor princess coming to a town of whom William Dunbar who penned the poem *The Thistle and the Rose* in celebration of the wedding, once had the nerve to write:

"May nane pass through your principal gaits
   For stink of haddocks and of skates . . ."

Even so, these "principal gaits" were decorated to receive the Royal pair, first at the West Port and thereafter at various stopping places where "trumettis" would sound and "maidinnis dauncit", before dignitaries of the Town would have their say in welcome. By the time the girl had won through to Holyrood she had had more than enough and four hundred and seventy years later one can still feel sympathy for that lass far from home. In fact it was not long before she was writing to her father to say that she, just as temperamental footballers do today—"wanted away".

But one can get used to most anything in time and apart from insisting that James shave off his beard, she settled down well enough in her new Palace of Holyroodhouse.

All was set fair once again—until Henry VIII came to the English Throne, in 1509. He resumed the "territorial ambitions" war with France who, menaced on her southern borders by Spain appealed for help to her partner in the "Auld Alliance"—Scotland.

James did not wish to offend his wife's brother (yes, Henry VIII was his brother-in-law and truly James would have agreed with the saying that one can choose one's friends but not one's relatives) and it is said that the Scottish king offered to renew the treaty of peace with England, made eleven years before with Henry VII, if Henry VIII would leave France alone. Henry took this appeasement move as a sign of weakness and instead of agreeing, demanded the use of the Scottish navy in his war with France.

James refused, and foreseeing aggressive moves in the offing, sent an ultimatum to Henry that if France was not left in peace, then the Scots would come south to prove that the attempt at appeasement must not be construed as meaning the Scottish army was not ready to fight . . .

Henry sent an army north under the command of the Earl of Surrey when intelligence reached him that the Scottish host was on the move . . .

The two armies met at the shallow hill slopes of Flodden just south of the Border. The military might of England triumphed. James had had a care for his artillery and his cavalry, but his infantry, fighting with their long spears as they did at Bannockburn, were out of date in the ways of war, for the longer English bill hook—a secret weapon at the time, cut through the ranks of the Scots.

King James and many of his noblemen died alongside the common soldiers of Scotland that day. One weary horseman came back to Edinburgh with the news of the battle. The old folk, the women and children of the Town, summoned by the great bell of St. Giles (which tolls the hours to this day— albeit re-cast) set about building a wall against the victors, but no invasion resulted, since no doubt the English army had not got off "Scot free".

A refinement of this wall begun in such desperate haste still shows in part—notably just west of George Heriot's School beside the "Vennel", that steep stairway leading to the Grassmarket. The east side of the Vennel way marks the line of the wall as it continued up to the heights of the Rock—the whole prospect the most impressive view of the Castle—denied to the visitor who persists in Princes Street.

9

"A little Love"

FOLLOWING the death of James IV, Scotland was again
on the brink of national disaster, with James's widow a Tudor
princess as Regent and the new king but a baby boy. Once more
a struggle for the Crown?

If the reader is growing weary of this recurring theme of a
minor succeeding to the Throne and the intrigue resulting,
bear in mind that Scotland was weary of it too.

However . . . apart from periodical raids from the south to
remind the Scots that they were under the heel of Henry—
which the Scots kept forgetting—this eighth Henry was again
so occupied with affairs in France that he found little time for
overinterference in Scotland.

James was a teenager when he ascended the Scottish throne.
As James IV's son he enjoyed the loyalties of the Highlands.
With such a situation, where he could turn his back on these
Highlands without wakening the next morning to hear that they
were in revolt again, he could concentrate in strengthening the
Border patrols and bringing law and order to bear, particularly
to the Capital where the College of Justice was constituted in
1532—and it has been doing a roaring trade ever since. (The

present Halls of Justice—the Law Courts, along with the old
Parliament Hall, stamping ground for the Law men of today,
are but a step from the site of that first place of Justice now
outlined in brass just west of St. Giles').

Young James had now to consider another responsibility:
the provision of an heir. He favoured a lady from France.
Consequently his security men prepared for headaches; but
Henry was again quieter at the time.

James sailed from Pittenweem the fishing port of the Fife
coast (and still flourishing) to where he had come from his
favourite Palace of Falkland (also still flourishing). James, being
young and knowing that the voyage might last some time all
according to the weather had, historical record tells us, two
barrels of sweetmeats and a cache of caramels included in his
personal luggage.

James married Madeleine, daughter of the French king, in
Notre Dame cathedral in Paris.

On the young couple's arrival at Leith, Madeleine, the new
Queen of Scots—"kissit the earth and thankit God that her
husband and she were cum saif through the seas".

Sadly, Madeleine "the fragile lily of France" died within six
weeks of her arrival and James must needs look for a wife again.
Nor did the tragedy of the first attempt dissuade him from
turning once more to France.

In time, another landing at Leith. The king's bride this time,
Marie of the House of Guise-Lorraine and of sterner stuff—
as shall be noted later.

James and his new Queen settled at Holyrood at the foot of
a Royal Mile now beginning to look more Royal than formerly.
It has been paved in part a few years before. Houses almost in
the style of Huntly House (built at the end of that 16th century
and now the Corporation Museum in the Canongate), were
taking shape under the guidance of the more ambitious builders
whose architectural aspirations must needs rise higher, since
they could not, on that now crowded ridge between the Castle
and the Palace, grow outwards—nor did they wish to, for safer
it was to stay within the Town walls when that man Henry
was still down south . . .

This habit of building higher and yet higher marked the
beginning of a housing development which was to become

characteristic of the Capital—wherein the lower orders occupied the lower floors and the hierarchy the higher. But in James V's time the new buildings of the merchants and the aristocracy were growing alongside cottages and hovels, still clinging to the sides of the ridge. The mixture was not yet shaken together thoroughly, except for, among other animal life, the pigs.

The pigs, neither snobbish or servile, roamed happily, nor did bye-laws and threats of fines of fourpence on their owners do much to confine them to their quarters. Thus can arise the picture before the mind's eye of a clattering warhorse carrying its proud owner up the Royal Mile suddenly shieing away—from a pig coming cantering muckily and erratically down the way, its floppy ears held in the fists of its rider—a small boy-heir to some noble house, squealing in unison with his mount.

Now James V was, like his father before him, a man of the people and liked to dress with their common touch on occasion —to get away from those very people—and the pigs. And wander free in disguise, either as a gaberlunzie (beggar) man or as the "Gude Man o' Ballengeich" which last fictitious title suggests he was better dressed than when in the gaberlunzie role.

In this way one day king James was loitering at Cramond Brig on the boundary between "Linlithgowshire" and "Edinburghshire". Was he the gaberlunzie or the gude man when set on by a band of men that day? Were they robbers—or close relatives of a maid who had been favoured by the king and this was he awaiting her appearance again? If the latter, then for sure they did not know that it was the king, these bludgeoners, since in these days, for a maid to be thus favoured by James, was an honour. Nor must his rescuer have known either, for when Jock Houison a miller, hearing above his corn threshing the cries for help, came into the attack with flail flying and scattered the assailants, he never thought that, as a reward for the rescue, for attending the man's wounds and giving him a draught of wine before seeing him part of the way back to Edinburgh, that he a modest miller would be presented with the surrounding Royal lands of Cramond in perpetuity, on condition that he and his descendants would always accord rest and refreshment to any monarch passing that way—a ceremony observed into the present time.

There are certain present day historians who argue with

conviction that although the ceremony is recognised by the Houison descendants for services rendered to the Royal house in the distant past, Sir Walter Scott did spread the James tale—that Scott changed the dates to suit his story nor did it all happen in the way described. This writer suggests with respect that Scott's version is vastly superior as a story to entertain. One thing for sure, since old Cramond Brig has been closed to traffic but allowed to maintain its ancient inscriptions of dates thereon when it was "repaired be both sheires", *there* is the place to invoke the romantic past—while above on the motorway to the Forth Road Bridge, traffic roars on to the Highlands.

10

"Sea shore skirmishing"

IN THE last chapter we left King James V returning to Holyrood after his incognito adventure: and we had given the impression that although James was wont to get himself into trouble in small matters, he was, however, running the country well enough with the aid of his loyal lords and his Queen Marie of Guise.

Alas, as they say in the better books, would that it had remained so . . . but the gloomy spectre of religious strife was rising on the horizon of history. Religious wars, which made antagonists of great monarchs of yesterday—and has done the same with little football fans of today—had begun.

And worse was to come, for certain noble lords of Scotland more concerned with their personal gain than the country's welfare and its independence and who craved to emulate Henry VIII's church treasure-hunting exploits, became the early agitators for a Union between Scotland and England.

James refused to consider a so-called Union and any imitating of Henry's persecution of the churches. Such refusals were fuel to fire the English king's ever smouldering aversion to the Scots and, also fearful that James might arm a force to harass

England while Henry was engaged in his latest war with France, first sent a body of troops north.

The Scottish king given intelligence of this, gathered together his followers and met the English force at Solway Moss. The Scots were defeated and the English could now turn undivided attention on France.

James, a despairing and dying man retired to his beloved Falkland where news was brought that his Queen Marie had given birth to a daughter in Linlithgow Palace.

A week later the infant daughter succeeded to the Throne—to reign one day as Mary, Queen of Scots.

In imitation of his illustrious predecessor Edward I, Henry VIII began what has been called the "Rough Wooing" of the Scots, in the hope that, unlike Edward who had failed in his attempts, Henry would succeed in fusing Scotland with England; and he proposed a Treaty which would put the young Mary in his care until the time came for her to marry his son.

Cardinal Beaton who along with the Earl of Arran first ruled as Regents, refused to agree. The Cardinal was strong for the "Auld Alliance" with France—young Mary was eventually sent there for safety—all of which was exactly the opposite to what Henry would have wished.

And so began the Rough Wooing, taking the form first of burning all the Border abbeys and then concentrating on Edinburgh as before. The Earl of Hertford who led the invasion force sent a report south telling how he and his officers had stood on the Calton Hill and watched the burning skyline of Edinburgh below, from where rose the wailing cries of the women and children of the Town.

As before, the Castle withstood the assault, but so thorough was the devastation of the Town that we are unable to resist the comment in the passing that had Hertford's men been less enthusiastic in their task, their descendants of today who invade Old Edinburgh (and welcome) might have seen an even older Old Edinburgh?

Mary, Queen of Scots was born in 1542. Five years later, Henry VIII died. Yet his presence is still felt in Scotland, for in visual form he can be seen on the main roads between north and south, his likeness emblazoned on a van: a figure wide stanced, arrogant and regal; yet sadly, he is associated with the manufacture of those crisps much devoured by the young:

>Sceptre and Crown must tumble down,
>And in the dust be equal made,
>With t'other modern Marks of Trade . . .

Now, some attention given for a lady who does not always receive her due—Marie of Guise who in many ways ruled the country while her daughter was safe away in France.

The Earl of Hertford, now Duke of Somerset, a power in the south land and a man of strong ambitions continued the attempts to persuade the Scots to have Mary married to Henry's son, now Edward VI. Marie of Guise would have none of this.

North came the Somerset man to resume the rough wooing, arriving at the Port of Leith after defeating a Scottish defence force near Musselburgh, to find—"the which all desolate for not a soul did we find in the Town". What did he expect? The seamen of Leith were already away on the autumn voyaging and the old folk and the children, forewarned were evacuees up the hill in Edinburgh whose Castle was becoming an increasingly powerful discouragement to any invader. Somerset contented himself with having the Leith houses fired and leaving a garrison on the island of Inchkeith for nuisance value (which garrison we are sure were delighted with their appointment) before setting a course for the south, being sped on his way when his men came momentarily in range of the Castle battery.

The garrison became a menace to shipping in the Firth of Forth and Marie of Guise who naturally had great faith in the fighting men of her native country brought over a force from France to help the home defence.

The French commander D'Esse a thoroughgoing military man, before turning his attention to Inchkeith, set about fortifying Leith. Twice in the 1540's, Leith had borne the brunt of the attacks on the Capital and her need for protection was long overdue.

Fortifications were completed—now for Inchkeith. Marie of Guise was there on the Shore at Leith to wish her fellow-countrymen luck when they embarked for the island—and she returned to welcome them back, victorious when the English garrison surrendered.

One might say the Scots are never pleased? Having got rid

of the English the growing Protestant faction began agitating for the removal of the French. Marie refused. Both sides prepared to settle the matter by force, and it was then that Marie decided to leave Holyrood and come into the safety of fortified Leith. Her Leith mansion was a sumptuous affair and for verification of this, look in at the National Museum of Antiquities of Scotland and view the carved splendour of her front door.

The Protestant leaders were for taking the Port by direct assault, but their military expertise being non-existent, the skirmish ended with the French chasing the attackers up the hill to Edinburgh.

And who do you think was waiting on the ramparts of the Fort to welcome back her heroes from the fight?

11

"Mary fair, from France"

EDINBURGH'S Port of Leith (a connection, the
Leithers in their independence of mind do still object
to) was, as mentioned in the previous chapter, fortified and
held by the French with the blessing of the Queen Regent,
Marie of Guise.

The Scots, and especially the Protestant faction, wished the
French furth of the Firth of Forth and the extraordinary
situation developed of the Scots *and the English* banding together
to fight the French on Scottish soil. It came about in this
manner . . .

That sharp shrewd redhead, Elizabeth of England now reigned
—like her father, a Protestant.

Mindful that the Scots Queen Mary was growing up in
France and about ready to come back to her native country to
ascend the Throne, Elizabeth saw the disadvantage to England
(sandwiched by the Auld Alliance) of Mary returning and being
welcomed by a French colony—and military at that.

With the Scottish Protestant leaders, Elizabeth made the
Treaty of Berwick in which she promised to send ships and men
and money to rid Scotland of the French.

Now, Marie of Guise makes her final appearance in these chapters. That redoubtable lady, mother of Mary, Queen of Scots, Queen Regent in her daughter's absence and champion of the French occupation force, retired to Edinburgh Castle before the Elizabeth-sponsored siege began.

The English ships blockaded the Forth and although in time famine threatened the besieged French, they never surrendered. Another treaty had to be made before Leith was a Scots-held port again. This was the Treaty of Edinburgh, or sometimes called the Treaty of Leith, and Elizabeth's secretary, the future Lord Burghley and an expert clearer of diplomatic hurdles, came north for the discussions. The fact that the French had lost their principal supporter Marie of Guise who had died in Edinburgh during the siege, gave the English-Scots temporary partnership an easier passage to a settlement—it being that the French should leave Scotland within twenty days and the defences of Leith be demolished.

All this, as if the stage was being set for the entry of a new and leading player in Scotland and Edinburgh's story—as indeed was about to happen. But before introducing the lady, an aside on one of her contemporaries—one of her enemies it might be said? Why did Master John Knox, once a religious revolutionary, captured at St. Andrews from where he was set to labour in the galleys of France, get his release from that travail by the influence of the *English* king Edward VI?

Edward, like father Henry, was a staunch Protestant who foresaw Scotland with a sovereign to hand who might also be heir to the English Throne—but from their point of view, having the wrong religion.

The opinion is put forward that Knox was a man looked on as able to influence this possible heir—and turn her *Protestant*. To *convert* her, just as the other Mary, Mary Tudor when *she* reigned, after her brother Edward and before the Protestant Elizabeth came to the Throne, tried so hard to convert all to the *Catholic* church . . .

A brief pause to allow the reader to work that one out.

*   *   *   *

An August day of 1561 and we are at Leith again.

Word has gone up to Edinburgh from the Port that a fishing boat has nosed through the mist to tell that the galleys of Mary,

Queen of Scots were on their way up the Firth. Too early by a day or two, which is why Mary's entry to the Palace of Holyroodhouse was delayed. Things were not just ready. In fact most of the dignitaries were not down to Leith in time to be of the welcoming party at the quayside. A good excuse would be the mist.

Enter John Knox, tough from his galley days, the man who refused to become an English bishop, the leader of the Protestants—and a loud man in protest: a reporter too, perhaps inclined to a natural journalistic exaggeration. Hear him now, writing in tune with the weather: "Never was seen a more dolorous face of the heaven than was at her arrival . . . the mist was so thick that scarce might any man espy another; and the sun was not seen to shine two days before nor two days after".

A thought for poor Mary, having spent her formative years in civilised France, and now, still teenaged, fated to step ashore to a mist-shrouded Leith still showing the scars of siege and invasion—and with John Knox glowerin' ower his notebook?

All things being not quite ready up the hill, Mary, with her four attendant Marys and her three uncles of the House of Guise were escorted along the quayside to Andrew Lamb's house where they dined. Lamb's House, symbol of the great days of the merchant princes of the Port still stands today, restored and given over to the welfare of the elder folk of Leith and well worth journeying down the hill from Edinburgh to see.

Mary now, to Holyroodhouse. And reporter Knox again: "At the sound of the cannons which the galleys shot, the multitude being advertised, happy was he or she that first must have the presence of the Queen: the Protestants were not the slowest, and therein were not to be blamed . . . Fires of joy were set forth at night, and company of most honest men with instruments of music, and with musicians, gave their Salutations at her chamber window: the melody as she alleged, liked her well; and she willed the same to be continued some nights after with great diligence".

Be it noted—"She *willed* the same. Will power to withstand the noise and a queenly politeness to please? And after "the same" was continued "some nights", did she open her chamber window and say in effect: "It's getting better, but you still need more practice"!

Spare a thought again for the girl from the fair lands of France, her ear tuned to the harmonies of the gentle lute, being subjected by her new subjects to the dolorous wail of fiddles in concert.

"Mon Dieu! All these Jocks and Knox too"!

12

"On being knocked by Knox"

IN THE previous chapter, Mary, Queen of Scots and
John Knox were introduced to the reader. They were
not themselves introduced to each other until later when Mary
was confronted with John as minister of St. Giles'—and capable
of bringing her to tears in some of his interviews at the Palace
of Holyroodhouse.

How did Knox go to these interviews? Did he come down
the Royal Mile from his manse in the High Street by coach or
on horseback—or striding down the causeway a black visaged
figure seen from the distance by the guard at the foreyett of the
Palace (you can still see the marks of the arches of this
foregate on the south wall of the Abbey Strand)? Then would
the guard turn and run into the forecourt of the Palace shouting

(in effect)—"Here he's, here he's, tell her he's here"!

Some years ago, religious views apart, the average male took Mary's side and scowled at the thought of that big brute Knox a browbeating of the little Queen. Now, as in many other instances, modern research has proved that Mary stood at six feet and Knox was a wee gnarled stocky kind of a man. Even so, listen to this snippet of him with the Queen as reported in his own *Historie of the Reformatioun* (after he had preached a sermon against her proposed marriage to Darnley).

Mary was in a "vehement fume" and said: "I offered unto you audience whensoever it pleased you to admonish me, yet I cannot be quit of you". Then, Knox writes, "he sustayned her Majesty's tiers"—or in simple modern Scots, "she started to greet". Knox replied—"When it shall please God to deliver you frae that Error in the which ye have been nourished, your Majesty will find the Liberty of my Toung nothing offensive".

"But what have you to do with my marriage" asked Mary, when she had recovered.

"God hath not sent me to wait upon the chambers of Ladies; but I am sent to preach", answers Knox somewhat obscurely. And so on, and on . . .

Enough, we suggest (with the spelling much modernised) to indicate that the Queen and the minister did not see eye to eye.

So began Mary's train of troubles—such as being accused of taking part in the plot to bring about Darnley's murder, when he was "raised from the ground with powder" and, apparently to make sure, was then strangled with his own garters "after he fell out of the air" beside the Flodden Wall just outside the Kirk o' Field where now, the south side of the quadrangle of the University of Edinburgh joins the line of South Bridge. That infamous incident only one of many in which Mary's name was implicated by the connivance of her Protestant lords—and one Protestant lady did not help either—Queen Elizabeth.

Long before the Kirk o' Field murder, even before Mary married Henry, Lord Darnley (who had private ambitions to become Henry the Ninth) Elizabeth was planning to have Mary married to Lord Robert Dudley. Elizabeth and Dudley were just good friends. He was a Protestant too, like the English Queen.

Mary's refusal to be dictated to in this way strained relations between the Royal pair. Ever present in Elizabeth's mind must have been the knowledge that Mary was in line for the Crown of England and—"a great coldness grew that they left off both from writing to the other as they used to do every week by the posts that passed between their Courts and Berwick".

That quote was from Sir James Melville's diary. He had been page to Mary in France as a boy of fourteen and was now a trusted ambassador. Mary sent him to Elizabeth to "renew their outwart friendship".

Elizabeth invited Melville to Westminster to see Dudley made Earl of Leicester. Elizabeth helped to put on the new Earl's ceremonial, he—"keeping a great gravity and discreet behaviour; but she could not refrain from putting her hand in his neck to kittle him smylingly".

Despite Elizabeth's wish that—"the Quen her sister should marry Leicester as metest of all uther" Melville left for Scotland with nothing settled. Elizabeth had shown a natural womanly interest in Mary, asking Melville questions regarding her appearance, for whatever the modern cinema has said, the two never met.

"She inquired which of them was of highest stature. I said, our Quen. Then she said the Quen was over high . . . then she asked what kynd of exercyses she used. I said that when I was despachit out of Scotland, the Quen was but new com bak from the Hyland hunting; and when she had leisure from the affaires of hir country, she red gude books, the histories of diverse countries and somtymes wald play upon lut and virginelis. She asked if she played well, I said raisonably for a Quen . . ."

Mary, widowed at eighteen in France, married Darnley. Widowed again, married the Earl of Bothwell. And with each marriage, it would seem religious strife and the way to civil war were ever more threatening. The common folk both Protestant and Catholic had their minds poisoned against their Queen, and in the end she was forced by her enemies at Court to abdicate in favour of her year-old son (to be James VI) who had been born in the Castle at Edinburgh.

Edinburgh was now well merged with the burgh of the Canongate. The ridge between the Castle and the Palace was crowded with dwellings. The spire of St. Giles' remained the principal feature on the skyline.

The crown of the causeway of the Royal Mile clattered to the hooves of the cavalry; the sidewalks echoed the calls of the pedlars, the marketing yells of the fishwives and the merchants' apprentices—and the ubiquitous pig wandered at will.

The King David Tower remained the dominant feature of the Castle defences, but of all the changes to the face of the Scottish Capital through the years, none was to be so sudden, so drastic, as that affecting the Castle after Mary abdicated—as will be told in the next chapter.

13

"Great guns!"

AFTER crossing the drawbridge at Edinburgh Castle,
the visitor will see, high on the wall on the left, and
just before reaching the portcullis gate under the Argyle Tower,
an inscription cut into stone and decorated with heraldic crest.
It reads:

> In memory of Sir William Kirkcaldy of Grange
> "justly reputed to be one of the best soldiers and most
> accomplished cavaliers of his time".
> He held the Castle for Queen Mary from May 1568 to
> May 1573 and after its honourable surrender suffered death for
> devotion to her cause on 3rd August, 1573.

Note the length of time he held the Castle.

After Mary had crossed the Border for the last time and to
exile in England, the country was ruled by Regents, and in
the period we are concerned with here, by the Regent the
Earl of Morton who had Scotland under his Protestant rule—
excepting Edinburgh Castle. Sir William Kirkcaldy of Grange
was of the opposite camp. To his mind, Mary was still Queen.

There are some aspects of the situation of that tragic time
that have become with the passage of some four hundred years,

liable to raise a smile. For example: what may be termed exercises to relieve boredom were instigated by Kirkcaldy; nor did it follow that he and his company besieged within the Castle for that long time, behaved by the book of rules, military. His soldiers would slip out to the Port of Leith and seize cargoes to stock the dwindling larders of the Castle. When the wind was in the right airt, down town would go a squad of the "besieged" to set the thatched roofs alight. And at times unannounced, a burst of gun-fire from the King David Tower would send cannon balls skipping down the Royal Mile. All that to remind the citizens and Morton's cronies in particular, that Kirkcaldy still dominated the scene—and as visual reminder, Sir William caused a cannon to be mounted high on St. Giles', of all places.

What, you may well ask, was Morton doing about this?

It was a question of finding enough of the Protestant persuasion to form a force formidable. Too much of the warrior material—especially in the Highlands, were of the wrong religion so far as Morton was concerned, and since Kirkcaldy's forays continued irksome to say the least, he was persuaded following parley with the Regent, to observe a Truce.

All quiet on the Edinburgh front . . . but awkwardnesses persisted. The Scottish Parliament held in Parliament House behind St. Giles' (and still existing as a parade ground for the men of the law) struck a snag regarding the opening procession of Parliament, which ceremonial was traditionally preceded in solemn column by Lords of the Realm carrying the Crown, Sceptre and Sword of State. Very awkward that, for the aforesaid Regalia was held by Kirkcaldy of Grange within the Castle (where it continues to be) and to save their public face Parliament had an imitation set made in brass for the occasion!

Stalemate continued. But Morton was a crafty soul and he negotiated, just as shop stewards and the like do today— except that he was in touch with none other than Queen Elizabeth. In previous chapters it has been shown that Elizabeth was not averse to helping the Scots, provided it was to her benefit—which meant not to Mary's—and she agreed to supply men and guns to end the occupation of the Castle by Kirkcaldy.

Now, whether the men and guns were longer in coming than Morton expected is not known, but what we *do* know, is that there was mutual agreement to end the Truce on the last day of 1572—and after warning the Catholic community to quit, Kirkcaldy opened fire on the Town as the kirk bells struck the hour before dawn on 1st January, 1573, the resulting cannonade sending fish baskets in the High Street market sailing scattered through the air, some of them finishing on the roofs of houses around. Indeed a rude awakening for many on that New Year's Day.

Thus, the mixture as before; the besieged garrison in the Castle resuming their guerilla tactics within the Town and using the line of the Royal Mile for target practice—to the extent that a great barrier of stone and turf had to be built across the width of the High Street as an early version of a sand-bagged defensive rampart.

And Elizabeth's men and guns? One imagines Morton grumbling away in his Town house or, to get away from it all, at his Castle of Aberdour across the Firth, muttering anent the laggard English force—"Uh-huh, uh-huh, aye ahint like the coo's tail . . ."

The attacking army did not arrive until near the end of April, presumably, come to think of it, because it was not then fashionable to war in the winter.

On the 28th April a trumpeter summoned Kirkcaldy to surrender.

Kirkcaldy's answer was to lower the flag of the Cross of St. Andrew on the battlements and raise in its place, the red banner implying resistance to the last . . .

Regent Morton and his officers in command, disposed themselves as follows in five battery of cannon: one where George Heriot's School now stands, another where now the Usher Hall raises its green dome to heaven, two by where even then a church to St. Cuthbert stood, and the fifth at what is now the junction of Princes Street with Frederick Street.

All this took time, this disposing (it will be noticed that no battery faced Kirkcaldy's main cannon commanding the Royal Mile from the David Tower, even although by this time the besieged's ammunition was much depleted)—and it was not until Sunday the 17th May, at a prearranged signal from one of Morton's guns, that the five batteries opened up simultaneously and, as the best cliques say—"all hell broke loose".

This concerted assault on the Castle continued for a whole week. It was the battery on the Princes Street line who fired the shot that finally sent the, by now, woefully weakened David Tower crashing down with its men and guns to the rocks below, the debris choking the draw-wells of the Castle. Yet, thirteen hours of hand to hand fighting followed before the surrender; and for Sir William Kirkcaldy of Grange—"death for devotion to her cause".

Regent Morton, by the grace of Elizabeth, triumphant—but left with a problem. He may have gained "face" by that campaign, but he had destroyed the face of the Castle. It was defenceless. What now?

14

"The last local King"

IN THE previous chapter, Regent Morton was victor
in the "Long Siege" of Edinburgh Castle—but a castle,
as a result of bombardment, defenceless: and in those days,
since one never knew who one's enemies might next turn out
to be, it was very necessary that the face of the Castle be
uplifted. As already mentioned and shown in illustration, the
King David Tower had been the main defence—but had
also been the main target in Morton's assault and it was on the
foundations of that ruined Tower, once the debris had been
cleared, that Morton caused *The Great Half-Bastion Round*
to be built—better known to us, but losing a fine phrase to roll
round the tongue in the process, as the Half-Moon Battery.

When one faces the Castle today from the esplanade, the
Half-Moon Battery dominates the scene. Note that below the
line of gun ports there is another—a single larger shaped
opening in the curtain wall from where the blast of a cannon
could suitably emerge: this lower gun port is the one that
framed the cannon of Mary's day—the main gun port of the
King David Tower—a survival from that "Long Siege". And

to the left of that Half-Moon Battery (as still viewed from the esplanade) the apartments, embellished and reconstructed, where Mary's son had been born. He came to the Throne, after the reign of the Regents, as James VI when he was seventeen.

This sixth James was a contrary character by all accounts. Well educated, but super superstitious—a witch-haunted man, lacking in kingly presence, yet keenly aware that he was monarch—a bit of an "auld sweetie wife" nursing the knowledge that one day he might be King of Great Britain if that Tudor wummin preceded him into the Great Unknown.

James did his best to bring the country peaceably together. An old chronicle tells: ". . . there in ye Palace of Holyruidhous, the King caused ye noblemen that had feud to agree togither; and after they had shaken hands and had drunken ane to ane uther, his Majestie caused them to come from ye Palace, every one in uther's hands, and his Majestie with them, to ye mercat crosse at Edinburghe, where ye City made them a very sumptuous banquett, his Majestie drinking peace and happiness to them all".

An extraordinary scene? The King and the courtiers cavorting up the Royal Mile—a Royal Mile which had been cleaned up a bit, previously, for the arrival of James's Queen, Anne of Denmark and Norway; when the below stairs pigsties had been camouflaged with tapestries and carpets! A Royal Mile with the beginnings of the shape of today. The Canongate Tolbooth and the Huntly House opposite were building. St. Giles' would be becoming increasingly like its present outward form of today—except that that exterior was wont to suffer certain indignities then, as witness: "The 10 of July, ane man callit a jugglar, played upon ane rope fastened between the top of St. Giles' Kirk steeple and a stair beneath the Mercat Croce . . . he rode down the rope and played souple tricks . . ." And leaning on the outside walls of the Kirk, the booths, locked at night—the locken booths or Luckenbooths which gave their name to a brooch still fashioned in Edinburgh. The most worthy booth of that time in both senses was occupied by a friend of James and a man who helped to change the face of Edinburgh too—George Heriot.

Heriot was a financier. A money lender and a goldsmith. A man to cultivate—which the King did, he being almost perpetually short of money. Heriot was symbolic of the dawn of an age of building and of business. The war-worn Capital was settling down. Fear of invasion was a nightmare of the past. Sober citizens ventured beyond the City walls. That street aligned with the Royal Mile to the south—the Cowgate, was now in aristocratic rivalry with its neighbour causeway up on the ridge.

The Cowgate may have been aristocratic then, but that democratic accord between master and man, so characteristic of the Scots, still flourished—how otherwise would it be acceptable for the Earl of Haddington of that time, nicknamed "Tam o' the Cowgate" by James, to rush out in his night cap and gown to join, as a former pupil, in a fight between the High School boys and students of the University?

The University is king of the Cowgate now—architecturally, for St. Cecilia's Hall has been restored by them as a concert room of Georgian elegance. During the restoring, a workman on the site told this writer that a huge pile of oyster shells had been unearthed in the surrounding foundations—a relic of the days of the supper rooms which the concert-goer patronised after the music. But we have jumped a century there to the days of the sedan chair and must return in time to the esplanade of the Castle some years after James had indeed succeeded Elizabeth and become James VI of Scotland and 1st of England —and had gone, some say with indecent haste south in 1603 to find a better bank balance awaiting him, and his share of trouble too, including Guy Fawkes in person.

Yes, the apartments where James was born, as viewed today from the esplanade, are much as they outwardly were in 1603. And another reminder of the days succeeding the King's departure over the Border: looking south from the esplanade, nearly every visitor it seems, singles out George Heriot's School as the building most worthy of admiration in the prospect stretching to the Pentland hills and beyond.

Heriot's School was the first and the principal of those in the City founded and endowed by him, originally—"for the maintenance and education of sons of poor burgesses of Edinburgh".

It is not generally known that scholars were not the first residents of George Heriot's however, for in 1650 true to their tendency to find barracks in the most unsuitable places—unsuitable for the owners that is, Cromwell's troops were billeted there.

How Cromwell arrived in the Capital would demand a complex explanation bringing in the Royalists and the anti-Royalists of both Scotland and England, the trials and tribulations of Charles I and Charles II in exile and the tragedy of the Marquis of Montrose and the Covenanting wars. Our concern here is with the Capital's story and simply to record that Cromwell came north to be Scotland's dictator.

In the next chapter we will tell something of his adventures in Edinburgh and district.

15

"The coming of Cromwell"

AS PROMISED in the previous chapter, here are
some further notes on Oliver Cromwell when he was
around Edinburgh. "O.C." as he was known to his men, was
indeed appropriately initialled, since, being already OC
(Officer Commanding) England, he had come north to try and
be OC Scotland, and succeeded to some degree—if anyone
ever succeeded for any length of time, in so subduing Scotland.
That Cromwell had to try, stems from the characteristic
contrariness of the Scottish nature, in this instance, expressed
by their religious convictions at variance with their loyalty to
Royalty. They disapproved of the monarch imposing his
religious views on them, but would cheerfully fight to the death
for his right to reign. And in Cromwell's view this would not do.

He came north by sea and landed at Musselburgh town, east
of Edinburgh, on a summer's evening in 1650, and after
arranging for the billeting of his troops he, with commendable
taste, had himself invited as guest in the village of Inveresk, to
one of the imposing mansions (still gracing that delectable
community) on the rising ground above Musselburgh.

(Some years ago, a skeleton draped with the threads of what

had been a Royalist uniform, with skeletal hand still clutching a primitive small bomb, was found in a secret recess immediately underneath the bedroom once occupied by Cromwell; which makes one furiously to think on how the course of history could have taken another path at such times— a train of thought on which Cromwell himself might well have pondered, had he known).

The morning following his stay at Inveresk, he gave the word for the advance on Edinburgh.

Which brings us, strangely enough, to Leith Walk, that broad highway between Leith and the Capital, for if Cromwell had not invaded Scotland, the Walk may never have existed. At that time, the routes joining Edinburgh and Leith avoided the moorland wastes between the villages of Bonnington and Restalrig (both now part of the City) and it was in these moorland rough pastures that Cromwell's opposite number, General Sir David Leslie had already caused a great ditch and rampart to be made as a defence; and as a place where the villagers around could come under the protection of Leslie's troops—also those inhabitants of Leith who lived outwith the Leith fortifications rebuilt by Leslie under the direction of John Mylne, one of the famous line of master masons who served the Royal houses of Scotland.

All Cromwell's Ironsides' attempts to break through this rampart were foiled by the defensive strategies of Leslie and the invaders eventually retreated to Dunbar to restore their energies after the frustrations of the skirmishes and minor battles around the Leith defences—and also to restore their supplies from their ships in the Firth.

Surprisingly, it was Leslie who made the next move, he having decided against all the odds to turn from defence to attack: and battle was joined near Dunbar.

Again, the course of history might have changed direction had not some of Leslie's soldiers disobeyed orders and impetuously rushed into the attack at the wrong time (not for the first or the last time in Scotland's history, either) and precipitated defeat. Thus after that strategic withdrawal from Leith, Cromwell returned in triumph to a now empty seaport from whence all had fled. Back came the inhabitants in time, however, when it was learned that a policy of peaceful co-existence was to be the order of the day. Co-existence is right, for when the Ironsides produced the first ever army newspaper in Scotland, among the announcements in time, were betrothal notices between the troops of the invading force —and the fair maids of Leith!

By then, Leith fort had been enlarged to accommodate the garrisons and house an impressive store of ammunition. Today, the arched entrance to that fort still exists, as does the rampart, for, after all had been settled and the rampart no longer of military importance, the top was flattened out and gravelled as a walk; in that way it became the 17th century equivalent of the Edinburgh Princes Street parade of today. But in these early days it was a walk (and "no horses were suffered to come upon it") on two levels, one on the rampart top, the other on the ground below: and in two instances this lower level still shows, most clearly above the position of the public library at the junction of Macdonald Road with Leith Walk where a house of two storeys stands on a lower level than the rest of the street— a house with a story of its own for it was once the home of the keeper of the Botanic or Physic Garden later to move and become the Royal Botanic Garden at Inverleith in the north-west of the City.

We leave Cromwell settled in Edinburgh with, as mentioned in the previous chapter, some soldiers and convalescents in the new Heriot's School; himself in Moray House in the Canongate; and his other troops disposed throughout the Town—a detachment in the Palace of Holyroodhouse for example and others, with that fine disregard for other folks ideas on what is sacred, in Trinity Church under the slopes of the Calton hill.

(The Trinity Church was moved when the railway came in the 19th century, all the stones being numbered before the dismantling against the time when it would be resited. These stones lay on the Calton hill for some twenty years before they were at last transported to the new site chosen near John Knox's House, but so many of the stones had been stolen or vandalised that only the apse could be re-erected. A Victorian addition to complete the church has since, in turn, been demolished, but the 15th century apse has been saved by the Corporation of Edinburgh and can be seen at right down Chalmer's Close in the High Street; and some of the numbers painted on when the church was removed from its

first site—near where the train now leaves the Waverley Station for London—still show on the exterior stones.)

Cromwell illustrated his slogan—"Trust in God and keep your powder dry", by using St Margaret's Chapel on the Castle Rock as an ammunition depot; and he acquired "the iron murderess" Mons Meg. And doubtless would have also taken the Regalia of Scotland (a bauble to him?) from that same fortress—if the Regalia had still been there. Why it was not there, forms the basis of our next chapter.

16
"The question of the Crown"

NOT ONLY, as we told in the last chapter, were the
Edinburgh approaches defended against Cromwell
before the City was eventually overcome by the Ironsides, but
news of his coming and knowledge of his dislike of the
trappings of tradition and the tendency of his troops to destroy
same, prompted the Scottish authorities to take the Regalia
(the Crown, Sceptre and Sword of State of the Kingdom of
Scotland) from Edinburgh Castle.

The Regalia were taken north and placed in the keeping of
the governor of Dunnottar Castle which, set as it is on a great
fist of rock out from the mainland cliff on the Kincardine coast
south of Aberdeen, was the ideal hiding place.

But, as Cromwell's domination extended, his soldiers came
north and besieged Dunnottar.

The governor and his lady realised that it was a matter of time
before the Ironsides occupied the Castle and discovered the
Regalia. And here, as so often in Scotland's history, it was the
women who dared . . .

Mrs. Grainger, wife of the minister of Kinneff had permission from the besiegers to enter the Castle periodically to visit the governor's lady, to bring wool for spinning and to carry away the spun cloth with whose weaving the lady passed the weary hours.

Imagine now, that you are on the cliff top of the mainland at Dunnottar on a day of the early 1650's. Seabirds scream incessantly overhead and against the silver gleam of the North Sea the great bulk of the Castle looms dark. A gate in its walls swings ponderously open and Mrs Grainger, hooded against the biting sea wind and voluminously skirted in the manner of the time, appears with her maid.

As often before, Mrs Grainger's horse is laden with a bale of cloth new woven by the governor's wife. Mistress and maid begin the crossing by a narrow grass-bordered path which first descends to near beach level then steeply rises in a curve to join the top of the mainland cliff—too steep for the horse to carry a rider; and not until the path levels out does Mrs. Grainger attempt to mount. She is courteously helped up by one of the Cromwellian sentries, one of a ring of soldiers—and of artillery, barring the way to Dunnottar. Then, Mrs. Grainger and maid set out for Kinneff, the maid trotting by her side, as anxious as her mistress to make a quick as possible move out of sight of the besieging garrison. They have seven lonely miles of moorland path to go and every so often cast a wide-eyed apprehensive glance back on the way they have come, always expecting helmeted troopers to appear in pursuit.

At last, Kinneff. The minister helps his wife down and all hasten into the manse. From her voluminous skirts Mrs Grainger removes the Crown of Scotland; from the bale of cloth, the Sceptre and Sword of State are taken.

That night by lantern light, Mr. Grainger buries the Regalia under the flagstones of the kirk floor, where they remained until the restoration of the Monarchy in 1659 when they were taken back to their honoured place in Edinburgh Castle.

Charles II had been proclaimed in London and had ridden into that City in triumph. Charles was also proclaimed in Edinburgh but did not ride into that City in triumph or in any other mood, ever. He had been prematurely crowned in Scotland but had had to hastily depart the country when Cromwell came north.

On now, to James VII of Scotland and II of England and further religious rows, and the plotting to bring his daughter Mary (known in her family circle as "Little Lemon") along with her husband William, Prince of Orange, to the throne. This was effected in England, but a hard core of supporters of James in Scotland led by Viscount Dundee at the Battle of Killiecrankie put up a temporary defiance in James's name.

As the end of the 17th century approached however, talk of kings gave way to talk of take-overs in the taverns and oyster bars of the Capital—of England taking over Scotland, or even Scotland taking over England. A merger anyway. A British Economic Community? As Big Business assumed command, so Edinburgh prospered; William and Mary's Continental connections (William by 1694 was actually king of Scotland as well as England) assured trade with merchants on the other side of the English Channel, meant also architectural exchanges of influence. Thus Edinburgh had, at the beginning of the 18th century ever new building arising—solid stonework from her local quarries but fashioned with the Continental touch—with the Dutch influence, as witness the gables surmounting the windows of the houses on the south side of the Lawnmarket. Here too, an example of the best in the Scottish tradition of around that time, in Mylne's Court, the first square in the Old Town; and this building best viewed from the Mound.

Happily unaware of the restive underground hankering after the Stuart line of kings persisting in the Highland fastnesses of the country (just as the common folk of Edinburgh were unaware of the underground plotting of those who hankered after a Union with England) Big Business marched on its triumphant way towards the Union of the Parliaments. For the last time, one winter's morning in the early years of the 18th century, the Regalia of Scotland were carried in the procession to the final opening of Parliament in Parliament House behind St Giles'. In May 1707 the Union was signed, and that morning the music bells of St Giles' which sent out harmonies across the roofs of the Old Town each day were ironically chosen to play a popular tune of the time whose words began with: "Why should I be sad on my wedding day" . . .

So, the Regalia were removed from their place of honour and

put into a chest in the Crown Room of Edinburgh Castle but with the decree that they should never leave Scotland. Also decreed, that Scotland should keep its own peculiar Laws and its own peculiar pound note; that a modicum of Members of Parliament in London should be Scottish and that Scotland should share the National—or Sussenachional ? debt. And finally, that in Scotland, the Royal Arms should show the Lion Rampant in the chief position. This last being observed for the first time about 200 years later.

But there was another Royal standard ready to stir things up again—that Standard on the Brae o' Mar—the Jacobite rising of 1715; but since we cannot keep harking back all the time on matters Royal or religious we will give that rising a miss and in the next chapter introduce a rising or maybe more accurately a riot, peculiar to Edinburgh.

17
"Monboddo and the Mob"

EDINBURGH crowds are much better behaved now
than they were in the 18th century—although one might
not think so on observing the behaviour of a wet-night bus
queue—as an actual bus hoves into sight.

A queue, of something even longer than a wet-night bus
queue, formed themselves into some rough order and marched
up the Royal Mile one evening in the 1730's to the sound of the
Town drum. A young man, newly arrived in Edinburgh and
just settling into his lodging was alerted by the sound of that
drum and the scuffle of the marching feet and stepped outside—
in time to join the tail end of the mob and satisfy a natural
curiosity regarding their destination.

To the shadow-scattering glimmer of torchlight, the mob
marched up the Lawnmarket and turned down the twist of the
West Bow on their way to the Grassmarket. (It may have been
quicker to go, not by the Lawnmarket, but via George IV Bridge

and Victoria Street? It *may* have been, had George IV Bridge
been built then, eventually linking itself to the West Bow with
Victoria Street; but a quick check on the dates of the respective
monarchs named in the titles of these newer thoroughfares will
give a clue as to the impossibility of that mob doing otherwise
than to follow the time honoured route leading in these days,
without any bi-secting bridges, all the way from Holyrood to
the Castle.)

Back to that mob then, which by this time had halted in the
Grassmarket and proceeded to their fell purpose of hanging
Captain John Porteous of the Town Guard (of which more
anon, from a hitherto unquoted observer on the preliminaries
to that event). Meantime, the young man, an unwilling witness
of the dread act, returned somewhat shaken to his lodging to
spend a sleepless night in whose small hours he vowed he must
leave this Town where the mob took the Law into their own
hands with such efficiency. That, in the light of day, he resolved
to stay, was fortunate for the enrichment of Edinburgh's social
scene as enjoyed in retrospect today, for the young man became
of the Law and, elevated to the Bench, took the title Lord
Monboddo.

In course of time, Monboddo grew to a rare eccentricity in
that age of eccentrics. He favoured baths—and cold ones no less,
and considered it undignified to sit in a carriage behind the
behind of a horse: he always rode on horseback, as he considered
a gentleman should, even on journeys to London.

Lord Monboddo was a keen hiker too. He would scorn such
as the sedan chair and this at a time when one of the sights of
Edinburgh was to see the Countess of Eglinton and her "braw"
daughters, each in her sedan, each attended by a gentleman
walking beside his lady with drawn sword, returning down the
Royal Mile by torchlight from an Assembly Ball in the High
Street. The only time Monboddo was known to hire a sedan
from one of the Gaelic carriers (the equivalent of the taximen of
today) was when it was raining and his way took him from the
Law Courts behind St. Giles', to his home in the Canongate.
Then would he call for a sedan—*to take his wig home and dry,*
while he stumped down the causeway beside it!

But we digress, or look too far into Monboddo's future when
he is thus discussed. Let us return briefly to the time of the

Porteous mob and to another admirable man of that age who was an observant boy of 14 years when the citizens of Edinburgh hanged the Captain of the Town Guard.

It is generally known that Porteous, after causing the deaths of spectators at the hanging of a smuggler, was tried, condemned to die, then granted a stay of execution expected to develop into a reprieve—and this last, of which the Edinburgh mob disapproved, with the result as above. But there was this boy in the congregation in St. Giles' at the Sunday service attended by the condemned before the day of their execution—in this case two smugglers; a profession then receiving a public admiration that is only given to professional footballers and pop groups today.

The popular version of the escape incident during that St. Giles' service makes a hero of Wilson who it is said spoiled the chances of his colleague Robertson in a previous escape attempt from the Tolbooth prison (the site now marked by the Heart of Midlothian fashioned on the causeway near St. Giles') by getting himself stuck in the prison window, he being the bigger of the two. Note that he was trying to get out *first*. To make up for this, Wilson is said to have forcibly held back the guards and shouted to Robertson to make a run for it from the church. But here is the version of our 14-year-old writing the account later: "The bells were ringing and the doors were open, while the crowd were coming into the church. Robertson watched his opportunity, and, suddenly springing up, got over the pew into the passage that led to the door in the Parliament Close, and, no person offering to lay hands on him, made his escape in a moment, so much more easily perhaps, as everybody's attention was drawn to Wilson, who was a stronger man and who, attempting to follow Robertson, was seized by the soldiers, and struggled so long with them that the two who at last had followed Robertson were too late. It was reported that he had maintained his struggle that he might let his companion have time. That might be his second thought, but his first certainly was to escape himself, for I saw him set his foot on the seat to leap over, when the soldiers pulled him back . . ."

The diarist was Alexander Carlyle, minister of Inveresk kirk near Musselburgh from 1748 until his death in 1805. In 1770 he was Moderator of the General Assembly and in 1789, Dean of the Chapel Royal. He was a broadminded man for his time. A theatregoer, a pupil of Madame Violante's dancing class in his young days, and then a student with a fondness for the billiard table—"which unfortunately was within fifty yards of the College". In 1745 at the age of twenty-three he joined the volunteer corps raised for the defence of Edinburgh during the Jacobite Rising, and although only an observer at the Battle of Prestonpans nearly fell foul of one of the Jacobite officers after the fight: this was Lord Elcho who—"had an air of savage ferocity that disgusted and alarmed. He enquired fiercely of me where a public house was to be found . . ." Lord Elcho was also a diarist; and some notes from his writing featuring Prince Charlie and Edinburgh will be included in the next chapter.

18
"A tartan take-over "

"BONNIE PRINCE CHARLIE." or, to give him his
non-tourist name in full, Prince Charles Edward Louis
Casimir Stewart, arrived in Edinburgh on September 17th,
1745: but Edinburgh had not been sure if they wanted the
Prince to enter the Town and had first arranged a parley with
the Prince's military council at his camp at Corstorphine near
where the Zoo is now situated.

While the City fathers were negotiating with the Prince, his
lieutenant, Cameron of Lochiel, with his Highlanders, slipped
away from the camp and made a detour in the dark to come up
by the side of the Town wall at the Netherbow Port.

(Pause here, for a little topographical note: the Netherbow
Port is no longer with us but at that time was the eastern
entrance to the Town, separate from the Burgh of the Canongate.
Today, the site is outlined in brass on the causeway at the
crossing just below John Knox's House. There are two
"portraits" of the gateway in sight of the site. One made as a

sign for the new Arts Centre next door to John Knox's, and one in stone, set high on the tenement wall a few yards down towards the crossing. The Arts one gives no idea of the original, but the tenement one does.

But to go back to 1745: Lochiel and his men waited in patience for the return from Corstorphine of the representatives of the City fathers' carriage which the weary, and as yet unsuccessful negotiators, had alighted from further up the High Street; and when it came trundling down to the stable in the Canongate and the driver stopped at the Netherbow Port to rouse the gatekeeper, so Lochiel and his men appeared. The half-wakened gatekeeper found himself with the point of a broadsword at his throat, and silently, the Highlanders ran through the open gateway to occupy, bloodlessly, Edinburgh in the Prince's name. Whether they continued silent is highly doubtful: a safe bet is, that despite the "gentle Lochiel" being in charge, the aristocracy on the top floors of the tall dwellings in the High Street, the merchants in their middle-storey abodes, the working folk in their pavement level rooms and the very pig in its sty under the stairs, would be roused by some pistol shots fired in Gaelic exuberance to the accompaniment of a chorus of Gaelic yells.

When the news was carried to Corstorphine that the Town (but not the Castle) was taken, the Prince moved in with the remainder of his Highland army—making a wide detour as Lochiel had done and well outwith both the Town walls and the range of the Castle guns.

Now, let David, Lord Elcho, eldest son of the fourth Earl of Wemyss and a member of the Prince's council take over as the Prince made approach to Holyrood from the ground under Salisbury Crags:

"The Prince got the news of Edinburgh being taken the next morning 17 of September. When the Army came near the Town it was mett by a vast Multitude of people, who by their repeated shouts and huzzas express'd a great deal of joy to see the Prince. When they came into the suburbs the Crowd was prodigious and all wishing the Prince prosperity . . . He continued on horseback always followed by the Crowd, who were happy if they could touch his boots or his horse furniture. In the steepest part of the Park going down to the Abbey, he was obliged to alight and walk, but the Mob out of curiosity, and some out of fondness to touch him or kiss his hand, were like to throw him down, so, as soon as he was down the hill, he mounted his horse and rode through St Annes Yards into Holyroodhouse amidst the Cries of 60,000 people who filled the air with the Acclamations of Joy. The Crowd continued all that night in the outward court of the Abbey and huzza'd Every time the Prince appeared at the Window. At night there came a great many ladies of fashion, to Kiss his hand, but his behaviour to them was very Cool: he had not been much used to Women's Company and was always embarrassed while he was with them".

After the victory at Prestonpans and the eventual move south, a reputation for anything but "Cool" behaviour with the ladies preceded the army. The English people "were Mightily afraid", and, to quote Elcho again—"when one of them was gott & ask'd why they ran away so, they said that they had been told that the army murdered all the men & children and ravished the women, and when they found themselves well used, they seemed mightily surprised. There was an old woman remained in a house that night where some officers were quarter'd. After they had supp'd, she said to them, Gentlemen, I Suppose You have done with Your murdering today, I should be Glad to know when the ravishing begins".

A final comment from the noble lord on that "60,000" who cheered the Prince in Edinburgh: "Not one of the Mob who were so fond of seeing him ever ask'd to Enlist in his Service, and when he march'd to fight Cope he had not one of them in his Army".

Doubtless Elcho's description of the huzzas and the kissing was exaggerated, as was his 60,000, since the population of Edinburgh at that time was around 50,000. Even although, after the Jacobite victory at Prestonpans when the Prince returned to Holyroodhouse to hold court, his presence cast a glamour over the Town, the majority were not for a Stewart on the Throne again—as witness Elcho's comment on the complete absence of volunteers for the army—for Edinburgh at last was settling down to business, to a period of comparative prosperity, to the promise of a "golden age" after a turbulent history. The wish was strong in the citizens to be allowed to get on with their own livelihood, comfortably aware that the reigning monarch was not down the hill at Holyrood but well out of the way in London.

Though many were unsure if the Union with England was working effectively (there are still many unsure) the last thing most would wish would be a resumption of the Royal and Religious troubles of the previous century. Some hint of this attitude is conveyed in another diary. Not by any Jacobite lord nor by a Royalist minister of religion but by an ordinary Edinburgh householder of that time—written by an 18th century relative of an elderly friend of this writer. When it came into the gentleman's possession he turned eagerly to the pages of 1745. There was not one reference to the Prince's stay. The "diary" was nothing more than a notebook devoted dully to the domestic and to dates, the highlight being the birth of a son into the family at that time of the Jacobite Rising . . .

19

"Knowing the New"

AFTER the Highland army of the Jacobite Rising of
the '45 eventually moved off south from Edinburgh, the
Capital settled down, with a sigh of content from the merchants,
a sigh of regret from the more adventurous of the maiden
populace and a sigh of relief from the Castle garrison, the
fortress under their care having remained inviolate.

Whatever these Risings of 1715 and 1745 had, or had not,
brought about, they did inspire a fine collection of song, never,
in Scottish history of song, surpassed—and popular still: strange
it is, to hear the sweet voices of a choir of the female English
regretting that "bonnie Charlie's noo awaa". And as a consequence
of reprisals by authority in the earlier of the two Risings, producing
too much spare time for the offender, the following prophecy
of the Edinburgh-to-be by John, Earl of Mar, resulted. He
was exiled for his part in the 1715 affair, in Aix-la-Chapelle
(now Aachen) and occupied himself in writing.

A paper written by Mar, reads in part: "All ways of improving
Edinburgh should be thought on: as in particular, making a
large bridge of three arches over the ground betwixt the Nor'

Loch, from the High Street to Moultray's Hill (the hill now occupied by the St. James Centre at the east end of Princes Street)—where many fine streets might be built as the inhabitants increased. The access to them would be easy on all hands, and the situation would be agreeable and convenient, having a noble prospect of all the fine ground towards the Firth of Forth and coast of Fife".

The Earl continues his uncanny visionary plan, suggesting there should also be—"One long street in a straight line where the Lang Gait is now; on one side would be a fine opportunity for gardens down to the Nor' Loch . . ."

To at least one visitor from across the oceans who recently remarked that she could not understand why Mary, Queen of Scots chose to stay at Holyrood so far away from the Princes Street shops, it will come as a surprise to learn that that famous street (the "Lang Gait" or Long Walk of Mar's reference) did not exist in the 16th century, nor, indeed in the middle of the 18th century!

Look now, for a moment on the Edinburgh of today: there, is the bridge of three arches—the North Bridge between the High Street and Princes Street. And if one stands on the slope of the gardens rising to the Castle esplanade to turn and look north across from where the Nor' Loch once lay below, one can see the original Princes Street of Mar's dream in the modest house-like buildings still at the corners of Frederick Street. Not that poor old Mar had anything to do with the practical realisation of it all. The principal practical one was George Drummond, six times Lord Provost of Edinburgh, Master of the Merchant Company, Grand Master of the Masons—another man of vision, and fortunate in that he had the opportunity—and the determination, to make his dream come true.

On October 1st, 1763, Drummond led a gathering of the Masons in solemn procession to the laying of the foundation stone of the North Bridge (the bridge that is pictured in bronze plaques on the parapet of its successor, the North Bridge of today). Drummond, opposing a body of the influential citizens who had a stick-in-the-mud attitude to the New Town project, persuaded them to give their support to the Bridge by explaining, with one of the great white lies of the century, that the main purpose of the Bridge was to facilitate transport and trade with the Port of Leith.

Unnecessary here, to go into details about the delays in getting the Bridge going. Even Drummond could not work miracles; yet a near minor miracle was performed on the New Town side before the New Town was there—or the Bridge finished for that matter: this was Edinburgh's first Theatre Royal built on the site now occupied by the General Post Office at the east end of Princes Street. A theatre had been planned in the New Town scheme and it just happened that someone with the true impresario touch had got in ahead of the houses.

Edinburgh has always had a reputation for theatre going, but enthusiasm has surely never reached higher than then, when my lady would be carried across in a sedan near the muddy foundations of the building bridge, the way, lit by link boys, their torches reflected in the marshy pools of the partially drained Nor' Loch.

But by the time Sarah Siddons appeared at the Theatre Royal in 1784—persuaded by an enterprising manager to venture north into this barbarian country where soldiers were employed at times to keep order in the theatre queues, the New Town was preparing to branch out in terraces and crescents, the envy of the architectural world.

The Nor' Loch, the stretch of water that had arranged itself so long under the face of the Castle Rock and all the way east to the district still called Lochend, had been drained dry; and here as an aside, another enterprise that got no further than the drawing board but is surely worth mentioning: this was a project to retain the waters of the Nor' Loch, to build a series of locks between Leith and the aforesaid Loch bringing a canal from the Firth of Forth up into the heart of the City. And that was not all: imagination took fire with the further possibilities; to extend the Loch to link with another canal leaving the City in a westerly direction (this one was built and called the Union Canal and is still with us in subdued form) which in turn would link with the Forth and Clyde Canal at Grangemouth (also still existing, just) to join with the Clyde. In this way, might a traveller have sailed up the Firth of Forth to the Port of Leith, then continued aboard on the canal by the series of locks to where Princes Street Gardens is now set and so, on to Glasgow without leaving the vessel; continuing, if the captain had a mind, ever west to the Wild West across the Atlantic!

Now, Edinburgh, at the end of the 18th century had her New Town and her link to the Old one. But everyone who was anyone did not automatically "flit" across the artificial mound of earth (now officially called The Mound which had been initially formed from digging the foundations out for the New Town dwellings) to the new place north of the Castle. No, the character of the Royal Mile maintained its grubby fascination, for as many men of letters and the Law who sipped the new fangled tea in the Georgian drawing rooms in that New Town, there were an equal number still haunting the howffs and oyster rooms in the wynds and closes. And of these gentry, crooks included, some mention in the next chapter.

20
"Captivating crooks"

IN the previous chapter we talked of the North Bridge.
Now, a word about the South Bridge—a continuation
of the other, but today, appearing as no more than a shop-
bordered street with the University dome in the offing—until
one glances down from this southward City way at a break in
the line of buildings, to discover below, the thoroughfare called
the Cowgate. This was once the southern line of the old Town
wall, once, too, a residence of the elite when the Royal Mile
could not take more, and this branching out on the then
southern extremity of the Old Town found favour with the
aristocracy.

The only aristocratic evidence left in the Cowgate today, is
St. Cecilia's Hall; a concert hall restored by the University to
its former Georgian elegance, at the foot of Niddry Street
where it joins with the Cowgate. A close look at this Niddry
Street (no more now, on its west side than the back of the
South Bridge shops) suggests archways underneath—and this
is so, some of the *nineteen* which form this extension southwards
from where the North Bridge ends.

There was once a Niddry Wynd (South Bridge demolished

it) and one of the characters who lived in that wynd leads us off to draw vignettes on three residents of the Old Town. One of crooked tendency, one quite a crook and the other a castigator of crooks but in himself too good to be true. First then, Lord Grange the Niddry Wynd resident, who did not get on with his wife, whereby he showed his criminal tendencies, even although a man of the Law, for he planned to get rid of her. There may have been some reason on his side since Lady Grange had the habit of standing centre of the courtyard of the wynd, broadcasting to eager ears around, and with fervour, a description of the less attractive characteristics of her Lord. So Grange had her abducted, employing Highlandmen to waylay her and bundle her into a sedan, herself suitably gagged, to begin a journey west—a thorough operation, for she ultimately was exiled in Skye with a stay on St. Kilda for good measure.

We do not think we like Lord Grange. Our second man, a professional crook, was a more likeable character He is associated with two of the most attractive groups of buildings in the Royal Mile. And he associated with two mistresses at one and the same time. This being a heavy drain on his finances, he resorted to gambling, which in turn, owing to losses at the gaming tables, started him on his career as a burglar, to end under the hangman's noose. Thus we introduce William Brodie, Deacon of the Incorporation of Wrights and member of the Town Council, whose father's house with the name still above the entrance arch enhances the architectural dignity of the Lawnmarket.

Brodie, in sober attire relieved with a touch of lace and a glint of silver by day, was transformed to a shadowed silhouette, masked and carrying a dark lantern in the black of night. He flourished undetected, working alone; his only ally, a lump of putty which he carried by day, surreptitiously taking impressions of keys traditionally hanging behind the doors of the shops, counting houses and dwellings he frequented in the way of his lawful business as wright and cabinet maker. (Robert Louis Stevenson may have modelled his Jekyll and Hyde on such a man and in the Lady Stair's House Museum a step from Brodie's Close, one can see a cabinet of fine workmanship by Brodie, acquired by R.L.S.)

Only when Brodie became ambitious and took on accomplices,

did things begin to go wrong. After initial successes such as stealing the silver mace of the University of Edinburgh, they turned their attention to a greater prize—the General Excise Office for Scotland housed in what is now one of the most impressive restorations in the whole of the Royal Mile—Chessel's Court in the Canongate. Here, fortune did not smile on them at all, for in the dark, a classic instance of mistaken identity develcped to a farcical degree between the two look-outs, a late returning Excise employee, and the two in the interior searching for the "treasure". There was then a general fleeing from the site without benefit of swag; and subsequently one of the gang turned informer. Brodie's arrest followed in Holland, to where he had flown.

The third of this trio, William Creech, must have raised pious hands in horror at such goings on. Creech, who had a bookshop at the east end of the Luckenbooths, that huddle of buildings once jammed between St. Giles' and the opposite side of the High Street, published an edition of Burns's poems. He took too long to pay the poet his dues after publication and this prompted Burns to be derisive in verse on "Willie"—a blow to the man's dignity, to one whose name appears in the long list flanking the entrance to the City Chambers, of the Lord Provosts of Edinburgh.

In 1790 the First Statistical Account of Scotland was under way and Creech was asked to contribute. He had the bright idea of comparing the Edinburgh of 1763 with that of 1783. A little exaggeration creeps into the Creech account. 1763 in Edinburgh, he approved; but 1783 in Edinburgh meant to him, the permissive society. In 1763—"five or six brothels, or houses of bad fame, and a very few of the lowest and most ignorant orde of females skulked about the streets at night". But in 1783—"brothels increased twenty fold and the women of the Town more than a hundred fold". Of 1763, "housebreaking was extremely rare". In 1783, however, "housebreaking theft and robbery were frequent. Many of the crimes were committed by boys whose ages prevented them from being objects of capital punishment".

Away from the crime count, Creech is more approving of the changes, for he remarks that in 1763 it took 12 to 14 days to coach to London whereas in 1783 there were 60 coaches each month and the journey was completed in four days.

According to contemporary prints, Bailie, and later Lord Provost, Creech was a pert dressy kind of a man and although bookselling was his forte, all manner of shops interested him. "Perfumers have splendid shops in every street. Some of them advertise they keep bears, to kill occasionally for greasing ladies' and gentlemen's hair, as superior to any other animal fat".

And the population of Edinburgh grew. In 1791, 80,000, including the suburbs; and in that category George Square and district where the University towers now rise, for Edinburgh was not only spreading north, but south.

And as tailpiece to this chapter, another population note: The Castle held in that year, 539 officers and men, 14 pipers and drummers, 1 barracks master—and 158 women and 131 children!

21

"Captivating comics"

WE HAVE talked of the eccentrics and the characters
who lived in the Old Town on the fabled Royal Mile
and perhaps given the impression that the New Town housed
none that were not the soul of sensibility and solemnity; that
those who had left the tenements towering above the High
Street for the Georgian grace and space across the valley to the
north and the sunny slopes to the south, were a class above the
old Town adherents and orthodox to boot. Not really. They
were the same folk. In fact, many of the male population would
have been content to stay in the old place but some of the
wives craved those higher ceilings, those wider streets, the
greater cupboard room and the air of gentility that went with it
all: thus, in certain instances a necessary nagging was brought
into play to win to that New Town, since, although the average
male dislikes the new, the average female glories in it.

Proving that oddities existed outwith the ridge between
Castle and Palace and in one instance in a village in sight of the
Capital, here are a few portraits. Take the village first. We put
the spotlight on Restalrig now part of the City and just beyond
the confines of Holyrood Park. Two claims to the unorthodox

here, although one of them does not belong to any category under discussion but we must include her for her very unorthodoxy.

This was Saint Triduana who lived at Restalrig long before even Holyrood was thought of, and who had come to Scotland with the pilgrims bringing the relics of St Andrew; then had retired to lead a life of devotion in the wild country inland from the coast. There, she was seen by a prince of the Picts who was well mannered enough to admire from a distance—and to keep that distance while his henchmen took a message to the lady expressing the prince's wish to marry with her, having fallen in love in particular with the transcendent beauty of her eyes. Triduana cherished her virgin state, but since this princely Pict had behaved so well in the courting and had especially mentioned her eyes, she was prompted to pluck them out, transfix them on a skewer and present them to the bearer with the message—"accept what your Prince desires".

In time, Triduana came to Restalrig. It would be pleasant to know that by some miracle she had had her eyes restored, for legend tells that long after she died, people suffering from failing sight journeyed to the well by which she had lived in solitude, to bathe their eyes. As a scribe of the 16th century put it in a wonderful journalistic brevity: "They came to St Trid's to mend their ene".

The saint in statuette surmounts the chapel by the parish kirk of Restalrig today—but there is no memorial of any kind to the other Restalrig resident who made *the first ever flight in Britain*. Yes, in spite of what the record books might say, James Tytler had the edge on them all.

He very probably was among the crowd who went to the grounds of George Heriot's School to watch Vincenzo Lunardi the Italian aeronaut who had already made the first balloon ascent in England, repeat the performance in Scotland. And yet, in that same year, before Lunardi's English flight, even, poor Tytler, hard put to it to maintain a growing family, with little time for his hobby inspired by a hero worship of the Montgolfier brothers (who had sent a balloon aloft in France filled with hot air, without human passengers but carrying some small livestock) at last had completed his home made balloon in the patch of ground behind his cottage.

He lit a smoking fire in crude imitation of the Montgolfier idea. But the fire, set in a rough representation of a balloon "basket" or "gondola" could not be persuaded to direct its heat into the mouth of the balloon and at last Tytler lost his temper, cut the restraining ropes and shot into the air. "And although he did not reach a greater altitude than 300 feet, nor traverse a greater distance than half a mile, yet his name must ever be mentioned as that of the first Briton who ascended with a balloon, and was the first man who so ascended in Britain".

About the same time, Hugo Arnot was pacing the New Town streets. He stayed in Meuse Lane off South St Andrew Street. An old lady who lived on the floor above his lodging, was often disturbed by Arnot's furious ringing of a bell when summoning his manservant. She complained, and at last he agreed to stop that way of ringing for his shaving water; and next morning fired a pistol instead.

Back to the southern side of the Town for another manservant episode. "Beau" Forrester lived in College Wynd (birthplace of Walter Scott and now named Guthrie Street, opposite the Royal Scottish Museum) and was attended by his valet at an open window, so that—"the barbarous natives might learn how a gentleman ought to dress". His toilet lasted three hours— and he dressed twice a day.

A valet again in attendance: this time on Lord Glenlee "scrupulously dressed in black" whom he would accompany from the Law Lord's home in Brown Square *(Now the space at the s.w. corner of Chambers Street)* down Crombie's Close across the Cowgate and up the back stairs to Parliament House. This little ceremonial morning walk was continued until Glenlee was nearly eighty—then his routine changed just as Edinburgh was changing, for now he was carried by sedan chair to Court. Not down to the Cowgate and up to the Royal Mile, but on a level way—along George IV Bridge.

To the New Town once more where, at 22 St Andrew Square, lived Dr James ("Cocked hat") Hamilton who might be considered the figure representing the link between the old and the new of that time at the dawn of the 19th century. He was the last gentleman in Edinburgh society to wear the old fashioned three-cornered hat, the collarless coat, ruff and knee breeches, with hair queued and powdered. He was a physician to the Edinburgh Infirmary and in his younger days a noted athlete. Even in his later years he was very active, for when at the whist table of Mr Ferrier in the latter's home at 25 George Street, and accompanied by his host's daughter in opposition to her father and Lady Augusta, daughter of the 5th Duke of Argyll, Dr Hamilton, when victorious, would snap his fingers, jump up, and career about the room, whereupon Mr. Ferrier would turn to his partner: "Lady Augusta, did ye ever see such redeeclus levity in an auld man?".

22

"What Scott sought"

AS THE 19th century grew apace and the Age of
Steam dawned with a murmurous and a terrible
foreboding (and a Scotsman was in the raising of that steam,
but more of him later) Royalty down south was discreetly
advised, as Royalty is wont to be, that it would be diplomatic
to journey north into Scotland—at that time, such a journey
something equivalent to present day Royalty making it to Tibet.

Thus it was that George IV, first monarch to visit us since
Charles II, sailed off from southern civilisation and landed at
Leith in 1822. And he did his diplomatic Royal best. He even
dressed as a Highland gentleman on occasion, but jibbed at the
bare knees; and wore the 19th century equivalent of the near-
modern pink "combs" or "long Johns" to clothe his knees, and
his nether limbs under the kilt.

Sir Walter Scott was one of the party appointed to entertain the king, and a visit to Edinburgh's Theatre Royal was one of the many successes of the visit. Probably the greatest success of the whole venture, taking the long term view, was George IV's agreeing to certain requests from Sir Walter to have this and that returned or rediscovered in Scotland—like rediscovering the Scottish Crown and returning Mons Meg, for the Crown and the cannon are now two of the major draws for tourists within the Castle. And travel agents can never be grateful enough to Sir Walter since he also put scenic Scotland on the map.

Always he did things in style. In 1829 Mons Meg arrived at Leith in the "Happy Janet" and, on a heavily reinforced lorry, she was hauled by a team of horses wreathed in laurel preceded by two lads in the tartan each carrying broadswords and mounted on a fine steed. The military escort was formed by the 3rd Dragoon Guards, gunners of the Royal Artillery and foot soldiers of the Highland regiments.

To the cheers of the crowds Meg travelled in this colourful procession the long way to Edinburgh Castle. The crowds cheered without knowing why—or maybe they remembered that vaguely heartening saying of the time—"Scotland would never be Scotland again until Mons Meg cam hame". A kind of a symbol of strength? As the Crown was a symbol of sovereignty? Of the fact that we were still a Kingdom?

But we are verging on the political and even unto the religious or nationalistic and must leave that to more serious heads and concentrate on resuming the role of an immature suspicion of the English: of the fact that, as mentioned in a previous chapter, the Scottish Regalia were put away at the Union of the Parliaments, although it was *said* to be decreed, that they should remain in Scotland . . .

Sir Walter again: Did he realise that the Regalia would be a fine tourist draw? Or did he simply wish to find out if they were still in the Castle? Considering what had happened in Edward I's time and what is still under the Coronation chair at Westminster, he might well be justified in wondering. To this end or the other he applied for and received permission to have the long locked Crown Room in the Castle opened, and a search made for the Regalia. Hear him in his own words:

"The chest seemed to return a hollow and empty sound to the strokes of the hammer" (the keys had been lost) ". . . the joy was therefore extreme when, the ponderous lid of the chest being forced open, the Regalia were discovered lying at the bottom covered with linen cloths exactly as they had been left in the year 1707".

The Regalia have since been on view in the Castle, except for the war years, from 1818 and that Crown Sceptre and Sword of State have never been better displayed than they are today.

Now, while we are at the Castle, a word about the time or one o' clock gun which initially had nothing at all to do with the military—and for the origin of the idea we must leave Scotland and walk with a Mr Hewat (of the Edinburgh Chamber of Commerce) who was on business in Paris one day in 1846 and enjoying a pre-lunch stroll by the Seine. He was startled by a loud bang. Then he noticed the monsieurs checking their time pieces and realised that it was the Parisian way of announcing mid-day. Why not, he thought, have Edinburgh, at that time checking one o' clock with the mariner's time ball on Calton Hill, announce one o'clock in this much more dramatic manner?

Mr Hewat contacted the appropriate authorities on his return. Ten years later the idea was accepted (they moved fast in these early Victorian days) and experiments were begun to find the most favourable position for firing, using the muzzle-loading eighteen pounders, still at the Argyle Battery and the first seen today on coming into the Castle.

This experimental firing was not confined to one o'clock but was shot off at different times of the day from different parts of the ramparts and at unspecified periods. All that, a disconcerting albeit stimulating shock to the nerves of the old ladies trotting along Princes Street below—until all was settled and they were only frightened once a day when the time gun began in 1861.

It might be said that that inauguration of the time gun marked the end of the old and the beginning of the new—the beginning of modern Edinburgh, for by that time the Capital was of the Industrial Age and making her mark in the worlds of brewing, of printing and of publishing. One man who linked the old with the industrial new was James Nasmyth, since he was born as far back as 1808. His birthplace at 47 York Place shows, at the street entrance, a plaque, including a neat representation of a steam hammer. It was James who invented it. Even at ten years old he was making toy cannon and peeries (tops) to sell to his class mates. As a teenager he had a small brass foundry fitted up in his bedroom. At 19 he had designed a "steam road carriage", thus becoming a pioneer of the motor car industry; and in time went south to fame (being received by the Czar of Russia)—and to fortune (he retired a wealthy man at 48.) Then he continued his hobbies of astronomy, of model making and pure science until he died in his 82nd year.

In the next chapter we must tell something of his father who painted the famous portrait of Robert Burns—a remarkable family, the Nasmyths, altogether.

23

"Edinburgh of yesterday"

AS promised, something more on the Nasmyths. James, the son mentioned in the previous chapter, was the only member of the family not an artist in the accepted sense. The others drew and painted with fervid application at 47 York Place and with varying degrees of success. But none with the success enjoyed by the old man himself. Alexander Nasmyth (1758—1840) was dubbed "the father of Scottish landscape painting" but is best remembered by his small unpretentious portrait of Robert Burns—the famous portrait so often reproduced, showing the poet's dark eyes aglow—just as they were remarked upon by Walter Scott, when he, as a boy, met Burns in Edinburgh. The original of the painting is in the National Portrait Gallery only a step along from the once Nasmyth home.

Father Nasmyth was also remarkable in being something of an engineer like his son James and had architectural aspirations—taking practical form in his earlier days, but of a visionary nature in his old age, when discussions with friends on what he would wish to see preserved and what planned for the architectural splendours in the Edinburgh of the future, were his delight.

If the ghost of old Nasmyth could return to his former home and look through a rear window he would see one example of the Edinburgh of the future in the shape of a concrete spiral rising to heaven: and would no doubt be intrigued considering his engineering interests and his son James's early experiments with motor transport, by the spectacle of the modern motor car ascending that spiral in the St. James Centre car park.

As Alexander Nasmyth in the 1830's pondered on the future of his well loved City, the Royal Mile was losing the last of its notable inhabitants. The rot was setting in—the acid rot of industrial smoke and the rot of property neglect. So, as the years of the 19th century advanced, where once a lady of fashion prepared for an Assembly Ball, a woman of the working class occupying the same room prepared for the tardy appearance of her husband's return from his Saturday night's carousal. Where once a Scottish Countess sat by a fragrant log fire, a huddle of bare foot children crouched by a smoky grate before being bundled into a communal bed.

In this way, tourists of Victorian and Edwardian days saw contrasts even more marked than any now. This writer's father knew an old man of over ninety who remembered in his boyhood in the 1850's getting a shilling from a tourist whom an antiquarian had brought up the winding stair to their working class home in the High Street, to admire the antique glories of their fireplace and mantelpiece.

But let not a picture of the Edinburgh poor give an impression of an all pervading destitution. From Victorian days until the 1920's by very virtue of the inhabitants of the Royal Mile being of the lower orders, life was real, life was lively. The High Street, the Canongate and the Cowgate to the south, were highways of raw living—particularly on Saturday nights, when a conglomeration of fruit barrows, sawdust-floored howffs, old clothes shops, broken heads, broken bottles, black eyes and bawling tartan-shawled wives brought a glory of near medieval crudity to the scene—enhanced when the citizens foregathered at the Tron Kirk steeple to "see the New Year in". Then, barrows heaped with glowing oranges, boxes of dates, tins of shortbread, all under the white glare of acetylene lamps slung from battens, made a living mural of light and colour down both sides of the street. Vendors with baskets stacked with paper trumpets, funny hats, comic noses, transformed many a sober citizen from the more austere districts of Town into a cavorting clown by the time the bell of the Tron rang out a solemn twelve—the sound nearly drowned by the cheers of the mob below, their sound in turn, drowning the muted screams of girls being kissed with some abandon, before all dispersed, pockets bulging with bottles, fruit and shortbread to "first foot" friends.

In the cold light of the morning after, let us take a look at this Edinburgh: at her face as it was, say, in Victorian days . . .

Old photographs of those times show a disregard for the face and even the roofs of the buildings, plastered as many were with advertising: the crumbling facade of John Knox's house spelt neglect; crude wooden slats of fencing surrounded the forecourt of the Palace of Holyroodhouse; White Horse Close was a slatternly slum; Chessel's Court a soot-drab gloomy tenement.

Now, Knox's house is a model of preservation—as are White Horse Close and Chessel's Court, and the Palace of Holyroodhouse gleaming in cleaned sunlit stone has its forecourt enclosed in wrought iron railings and gateways of a magnificence appropriate where once wooden fencing stood askew. And such thoughts on how restoration has advanced are a comfort and a consolation to our councillors in the City Chambers of the Capital suffering the cannonades of criticism shot at them by citizens on why this and that has not been done, on what should be undone, and when is so and so going to be done and etc.

Much more would have been done earlier, on the slums of the Royal Mile except that on an autumn day of 1939 the citizens of Edinburgh watched wheeling aircraft and anti-aircraft shell bursts adorn the sky and were innocently unaware that they were witnessing the first air raid on Britain in the second World War when enemy aircraft attacked the Forth Railway Bridge.

When peace came, the war on Edinburgh's slums was renewed. Fisher's Close in the Lawnmarket with its Flemish style gables was in such a state that every time the one o'clock gun was fired parts of the ceilings pattered to the floor. Now Fisher's Close is restored and so the good work continues: the

facades of the old buildings emerge as they appeared in
Edinburgh's "Golden Age" but inside there has been trans-
formation. Thus the wheel has turned full circle . . . Where
once a Countess pondered the problems of ablution and later,
where a poor woman huddled with her barefoot bairns at a
smoky grate, a modern business girl luxuriates in the warm
privacy of a fragrant bath in her well-appointed flat. A patina
of respectability has descended on the Royal Mile but the
ghost of the roistering days of sword thrust and intrigue are
still around for the imaginative and the best way to raise such a
ghost might be referred to in the next and final chapter.

24

"Edinburgh of today"

A strange coincidence that as I fitted the sheet into the typewriter for this, the final chapter, the radio, which I was about to switch off, announced that Ian Whyte's tone poem "Edinburgh" was now to be played—so I listened (a first hearing for me) and even heard as promised by the announcer, the subtle effect of the sound of the distant one o'clock gun from the Castle.

Listening to this poem in sound cancelled out how I intended to write the beginning of this chapter, for Ian Whyte, once the conductor of the BBC Scottish Symphony Orchestra, being a musician and composer of quality, his tone poem was a reminder of the timeless quality of Edinburgh and decided me not to be facetious about the things that were wrong with the City today, but dwell on the Edinburgh that no yellow parking lines (as forecast by the old seer in the first chapter) nor concrete cliff of modern times can spoil.

One further word on the broadcast. The item before the Edinburgh one happened to be Hamish McCunn's "Land of the Mountain and the Flood" (the title from Scott, with the word "flood" meaning not a devastation but a fine flowing pre-Hydro-electric-days river with full blooded falls). Such a piece with its noble use of trumpet and horn, might be termed a tone poem on Scotland.

In that way, by chance, two items of music were heard acting as a prologue to this *Scotland's Capital* epilogue, for as the reader who has lasted the pace will have noticed, these first chapters began (half-fiction half-fact) by almost telling the early story of Scotland when Edinburgh was in its infancy and elements beyond its boundaries were explained as fashioning its future—then all was fined down to concentrate on the facts of the City itself. In this way, then, not only can all these passing 25,000 words spanning 1000 years of history be said to be about Scotland's Capital, but in part, about Scotland. Thus, our title can also be a statement too—if we take away the apostrophe, for then it can also read: SCOTLAND IS CAPITAL.

But enough of this sly trumpet blowing for our native country. Let me go with you for a final tour of what happens to be my native city, around a few of the places not featured in the guide books.

We'll begin at the Castle (where else ?). Come early and literally avoid the rush if you are, like the swallow, a summer visitor. Find, or ask to see the sculpture of the gas-detecting mice of World War 1 who have their little place of honour in the Scottish National War Memorial. Note that other piece of sculpture under the arch at the drawbridge showing the "portrait" of Mons Meg. And when you are leaving the Castle and turn to photograph it from the esplanade, don't omit to try one from the south wall of the esplanade showing the rock descending and thus avoid having a large expanse of foreground esplanade making the bulk of the Castle more than somewhat diminished. (If the stands are up for the Tattoo however, this may be found too difficult to realise.)

Down the Lawnmarket now and look in at Riddle's Court for a picture of domestic architecture of varied periods in Edinburgh's story.

Now, the High Street: whether or no you go into St. Giles', go round to its rear and enter Parliament House so often missed by the Royal Mile trekker. If the Courts are sitting, then the pacing be-wigged law men will add to the atmosphere of once-upon-a-time. This place is notable as the interior from which this writer was escorted by officialdom when he attempted to draw there without permission—the explanation of his dismissal being that if he were allowed, everyone would be in there with their sketch books. One look at the elaborations of the hammer beam ceiling makes nonsense of such an excuse—but I forgive and turn the other cheek so to speak to advise a visit—especially on some morning when Scotch mist wreaths the spires and turrets of the City, for inside there is warmth of colour and animation and red-robed judges and portraits of fleshly and forbidding countenance.

The Old Town atmosphere does not really begin again until we are passing John Knox's house, for the Canongate has the architectural edge on the High Street now—and if you are interested in heraldry, you should go in to see the Royal pews in the Canongate kirk.

You have a camera and wish a view of the Old Town? After finding the three faces with but four eyes between them, on the fountain of the forecourt of the Palace of Holyroodhouse, enter Holyrood Park and climb up the turfed path *on top* of the crags until you come to a "V" shaped gully called the "Cat's Nick" at the head of this line of precipice. This rocky "V" acts as a frame for a prospect of the Old Town particularly effective in an evening light.

If, after a return to Holyrood, the Royal Mile is not wanted as a repeat performance, go all the way by Holyrood road and the Cowgate to the Grassmarket, and take a step up the Vennel to its south-west corner, for here, and around the West Port, are views of the Castle far removed from the Princes Street shortbread-lid picture of popular appeal: here, appears a *real* Castle with the rock towering above the tenements. And a good way back to the tourist track is by the north side of the Grass-market and up the West Bow and Victoria Street, for that way exists now, as a variegated window-gazing glory.

Thistle Street between Frederick Street and Hanover Street too, for shop windows rich and strange—and now that we have shot over to the New Town, savour George Street on an evening stroll or Heriot Row by Queen Street Gardens where the little round pond with miniature island was said to have been the inspiration for a small boy who played there and grew up to write *Treasure Island* . . . savour such streets in the dusk of a still autumn evening and you'll raise the kindly ghosts of the 18th century.

A goodbye now, to Edinburgh from one of her viewpoints. From the top floor of the Gallery of Modern Art in the Royal Botanic Garden—or if one goes to the Zoological Park and leaves by the hill road at the summit, the view of the City from Corstorphine Hill at which place in Robert Louis Stevenson's *Kidnapped* Alan Breck says goodbye to David Balfour—and here they say goodbye, to you.